Where's Noah?

A Lenten Program
Of Services And Activities

Arley K. Fadness

CSS Publishing Company, Inc., Lima, Ohio

WHERE'S NOAH?

*To my parents — Elenora and the late Lawrence Fadness — my sister Oriette,
my brothers Gary and Marlowe, and to my faith families —
Bethesda Lutheran in Bristol, South Dakota; Bethel Lutheran of Phoenix, Arizona;
Volin Parish at Volin, South Dakota; English, Diamond Lake, and Grace at Lake Benton, Minnesota;
Salem Lutheran at Parkston, South Dakota; Beaver Creek, Springdale, and Shalom at Harrisburg,
South Dakota; and Messiah Lutheran at North Mankato, Minnesota.*

Copyright © 2000 by
CSS Publishing Company, Inc.
Lima, Ohio

The original purchaser may photocopy material in this publication for use as it was intended (i.e., worship material for worship use; educational material for classroom use; dramatic material for staging or production). No additional permission is required from the publisher for such copying by the original purchaser only. Inquiries should be addressed to: Permissions, CSS Publishing Company, Inc., P.O. Box 4503, Lima, Ohio 45802-4503.

Some scripture quotations are from the *New Revised Standard Version of the Bible*, copyright 1989 by the Division of Christian Education of the National Council of the Churches of Christ in the USA. Used by permission.

Some scripture quotations are from the *Good News Bible*, in Today's English Version. Copyright © American Bible Society 1966, 1971, 1976. Used by permission.

ISBN 0-7880-1557-5   PRINTED IN U.S.A.

Preface

For seven weeks Messiah Lutheran Church in North Mankato was cheered with the sounds of children, moms, dads, and grandparents learning, growing, sharing, and worshiping together around the theme *Where's Noah?*

Lent 1997 saw senior citizens interact with children as they made and distributed wooden animal tokens during the "Mister Noah" time.

Mister Noah, proud of his costume and helmswheel, appeared each week with a message that served as a prelude to the homily by the pastor.

A special original song written by Jeff Callander, "When the Rain Came Down," quickly became a favorite.

Brief, pithy sermons directed the hearers to the themes of baptism, sin, redemption, environmental preservation and caring for others.

Worshipers smiled but caught the distinction between the secular and sacred when Simon Peter and Peter Cottontail met in the Garden of Resurrection on Easter morning.

Introduction

We are embarking on a quest to find "Noah" — Noah of the Holy Bible. As we seek to discover the person, the life, and unique experiences of Noah, this Old Testament legendary character, we will more clearly define and understand ourselves. We will find we are people caught in the web of sin, rescued and preserved in our Baptism covenant relationship with God through Christ, and called to obedience. We will see ourselves in Noah as preservers of creation and as God's contemporary environmentalists, stewards of the earth, conservers of endangered animal species, and champions for an improved quality of life. We, like Noah, are called to be builders of Arks and Altars.

Where's Noah? is an intergenerational Lenten series that stresses that Lent is for children too, that all ages may be involved in the production, implementation, and participation of this ministry, and that all spiritual gifts are tapped and needed.

It is a fact: **"It takes an Ark to save a child."**

Table Of Contents

Mister Noah Monologues (Seven monologues, 3-4 minutes each)	7
Lenten And Holy Week Meditations	
Where's Noah? In The Swill	14
Where's Noah? On The Path Of Faithfulness	17
Where's Noah? Building An Ark And An Altar	19
Where's Noah? Saved On The Ark	21
Where's Noah? Receiving A Rainbow	23
Where's Noah? Near The Saving Flood (Baptism)	25
Where's Jesus? In The Upper Room	27
Where's Jesus? At Golgotha	29
Where's Jesus? In The Resurrection Garden	32
Versicle For Opening Liturgy	35
Thematic Folk Song, "When The Rain Came Down" by Jeff Callander (with lyrics and chords)	36
Noah's Ark Wooden Animal Tokens Sample Instructions	39
"Noah" Character Instruction Guide	40
Home Family Time Crossword Puzzles	41
Invitational Sample Letter To Parents From Your "Loving Child"	53
Preparations For Holy Communion On Maundy Thursday	54
A Bible Study On Genesis 6-9	55
Monologues For Women In The Upper Room	59
Sample Bulletins	63
Original Easter Sunrise Play: "Alive! An Easter Play" featuring Peter Cottontail and Simon Peter	72
Outline For Screen Projection Option	76

Sample Promotional Page

Where's Noah?
Is The Theme for Lent This Year!
You are WELCOME to our Lenten Worship Series
Wednesdays in Lent at 7:30 p.m.

Themes for Lent are:
- (Date) Where's Noah?
  In The Swill
- (Date) Where's Noah?
  On The Path Of Faithfulness
- (Date) Where's Noah?
  Building An Ark And An Altar
- (Date) Where's Noah?
  Receiving A Rainbow
- (Date) Where's Noah?
  Near The Saving Flood (led by youth)
- (Date) Holy Week — Passion Sunday
- (Date) Maundy Thursday
  Where's Jesus?
  In The Upper Room
- (Date) Good Friday
  Where's Jesus?
  At Golgotha
- (Date) Easter
  Where's Jesus?
  In The Resurrection Garden

A Noah character (member John Doe) will be present during this Lenten series at the "Mister Noah" time to assist in worship and be available to talk to children and adults.

Children will collect "Noah's Ark" animal tokens during these Wednesday evening worships in Lent. Some of our older members are busy preparing these tokens.

A special theme song: "When The Rain Came Down" written by Pastor Jeff Callander and projected on our screen will tell the Noah story in song.

Children and parents will work together on "Noah" projects for learning and bonding.

Lent begins (date) on Ash Wednesday.

5:30 p.m. Classes begin
7:30 p.m. Worship begins

Ash Wednesday

Where's Noah?
In The Swill

Mister Noah Time
Number One

("Noah" greets the children prior to Lenten worship in the narthex and gives them their first animal token as they go into the Lenten worship. "Noah" serves as the Lector in this worship. He sits in a fairly prominent place.)

Good evening. I'm Noah from the Old Testament. You find me in the Book of Genesis, chapter five, verse 20, to chapter 10, verse 32.

You may know me. You might not know me. I'm here. I'm there. I'll be everywhere in the next forty days. Forty days? Hmmmmm. Forty? Forty? Forty!

(Holds up a big "40" prop.)

I'll bet you Bible scholars know why this is important. Or do you? In the next forty days, who knows *where* I'll be? Who knows *what* I'll be doing?

And you know what? Everybody, yes, everybody, is going to ask, "Where's Noah?" *(Laughs mischievously.)*

Tonight, I'm your lector. The lessons are found in Genesis, Joel, and Matthew.

(Reads Genesis 6:1-7; Joel 2:12, 13; and Matthew 24:27-39.)

Lent 2

Where's Noah?
On The Path Of Faithfulness

Mister Noah Time
Number Two

(Noah may be positioned near a helmswheel prop. He may wear a captain's hat.)

Hi ya, mates! Hey there, all you landlubbers. I'm Mister Noah — Captain Noah, if you please, and I run this ark. I want all you boys and girls aboard. C'mon.

(Traveling music such as a sea chantey while the children are assembling around Captain Noah.)

I'm Noah of Noah's Ark. You know the story! Glad, super glad to have you aboard.

Actually, my ark isn't quite finished yet. People thought I was crazy to build this ship right here in the desert. Did it because God said so. And when God talks, I listen. Do you listen when God talks to you through the Holy Bible and the Sacraments? If you're smart you will. Only the foolish ones don't.

Say, boys and girls, see what I have here. A letter of the alphabet. *(Shows letter "F.")* You know this letter? If it's your grade in school would you like it? You know, "F" has had kind of a bad rap. It's a really great letter. It's great because it stands for Faith and Faithfulness. That's the topic the pastor is going to preach about tonight — faithfulness.

Oh, I love hearing my pastor(s) preach God's word. Don't you?

But now let me tell you, it really humbles me to hear what the Bible says about *me*. Says *I* found favor in the sight of God. God considered me faithful. Wow!

Really, boys and girls, it's the Holy Spirit that gives faith. Faith is a gift. We are able to trust God only by throwing our entire weight on the Lord.

Faith is like diving into the water and believing that the water won't drown you but hold you up. "For by grace are you saved through faith," the Bible teaches.

Well, thanks, boys and girls. Gotta' end Mister Noah Time. Here's a little item for your ark collection.

(Passes out animal tokens.)

See you next week.

(Traveling music.)

Lent 3

Where's Noah?
Building An Ark And An Altar

Mister Noah Time
Number Three

Hi, all you land lovers. C'mon up boys and girls. Gotta' tell ya some stuff. Won't be long and I'll be sailing!

(Traveling music; children assemble.)

Nope, I'm not going sailing on the Minnesota River. Not Lake Washington. Not even Lake Superior. Bet you'll never guess.

My neighbors think I'm looney. *(Makes looney faces and sounds)* Nope, I'm as sane as can be. I was told there's a flood acomin'.

Yep, that's what I said. I know it's kinda hard to believe. But it's a'coming, sure as God said it would. Oh my.

Now next week I want you to bring something special for the voyage. I want you to bring a pretend animal like this. *(Shows teddy bear, or any other stuffed animal.)* Bring a cow, a giraffe, any pretend animal you've got. I'll pray a prayer of blessing and talk to you about how important it is for us to preserve the animals — especially the endangered species.

When God created the world and animals and all — God said, "It is good!" Today a new flood of hunger and poverty and environmental destruction threatens to destroy the earth and its creatures.

Will you help me by being good stewards of the earth and will you help me save the animals?

Now, here's a token from my ark. *(Passes out animal tokens.)* It's important to collect the whole set.

Now it's time for me to disappear 'til next time.

'Bye, boys and girls. 'Bye, all. *(Waves.)*

(Traveling music.)

Lent 4

Where's Noah?
Saved On The Ark

Mister Noah Time
Number Four

Captain Noah here, of the S.S. Ship Ark. I want all you boys and girls to come up to the Captain's deck. I've got something for you.

(Children assemble to traveling music.)

Did you bring your pretend animals? See, I've got mine. *(Shows stuffed animals of various kinds and places them strategically.)* Oh my, look at what we have. *(Admires, ogles, and fawns over the animals, asks questions, and so forth.)*

Not only did God save me, my wife, my three sons, and their wives on the ark from the waters of that angry flood but also all these animals. In your book of Genesis you can read about how God created everything on this earth and it was good! God wants to preserve his creation, not destroy it.

I love animals, don't you? My favorite animal is a _____ because _____.

You know, boys and girls, God wants you to be saved too from the flood of sin and evil. Jesus is the one who saves. From the day you were baptized Jesus says, "I want to live in your life always. I saved you on the cross. I love you. I died for you."

And God loves animals, too. God wants us to care for the earth, be responsible stewards, save the endangered species, clean up the water, air, rivers, and mountains, and the birds in the tree tops on Mocking Bird Hill. It's a big job but we can do it, can't we? Let's pray to God for guidance and help.

Prayer:
Lord, you created us and also this amazing world. You came in Jesus to save us from our sins and to save all that you have made. Bless all your creatures great and small and make us preservers of life as was Noah. In Jesus' name. Amen.

(Passes out animal tokens as children are dismissed. Traveling music.)

Lent 5

Where's Noah?
Receiving A Rainbow

Mister Noah Time
Number Five

Hello, boys and girls, moms and dads, too.

C'mon up and join me. I'll bet you've been wondering where I have been. Well, you know you could find me here at (Messiah Lutheran) Church this Lenten Season. I'm so glad to be here. I've got something really important to share with you.

(Traveling music as children assemble.)

After God saved me and my wife; my three sons, Ham, Shem, Japtheth, and their wives, God gave me a wonderful gift. Not only did God give me and the world a wonderful promise that God would not destroy humans or any living creature again but God also gave a beautiful rainbow as a sign. I love rainbows, don't you?

(Talk about or display a colorful rainbow.)

How many of you have seen a rainbow lately? Every time I look up and see one, I know that's God's sign that God's word is true and totally dependable.

Now I'm giving you God's rainbow. It's not only mine but yours, too. And you and I are to be God's Rainbow People. Know what it means to be a "Rainbow Person"? It means that you are to share Jesus' promises with people who are needy or lost or feel hopeless.

It means that you are to care for God's living creatures — that's animals and reptiles and amphibians and plant species and the rain forest. You are a Rainbow Person whenever you help a poor person or tell someone about Jesus or when you don't litter and ruin the environment.

Well, it's been fun, boys and girls. I've gotta' say 'bye for now. Don't forget your ark tokens.

(Passes out animal tokens.)

God loves you and so do I.

(Traveling music.)

Lent 6

Where's Noah?
Near The Saving Flood (Baptism)

Mister Noah Time
Number Six

Good evening, you all. Noah here — and you will notice I am standing right by the baptismal font in your church. As you children come up I want you to think about why I am standing here instead of at the helmswheel.

(Traveling music.)

I'm so glad to see you boys and girls. I'm standing near the baptismal font where some of you were baptized. And you know what? I found some liquid in the font.

(Dip hand in water and splash it around — sprinkle on children.)

What is it? Is it Seven-up? Is it clear liquid soap?

Nope, none of those.

(Children give answer.)

Yep it's water. And I've had a lot of experience with water. Bad water. Drowning water. But you know what? This is good water. This water is a friend, not an enemy. In the flood you remember the water drowned the people, animals, birds, and vegetation, but God saved me and my family and a lot of other living things. And so it is, that water not only kills, but gives life.

And water connected to the Word of God gives us life by connecting us to the life, death, and resurrection of Jesus. Jesus saves us. And baptism is the beginning of that new life. Of course, remember as Martin Luther taught us, it's not the water only, but most importantly God's word that rescues us from drowning in sin, from death and the power of the devil.

You've got a lot to celebrate. Your baptism!

(Light a baptism candle.)

Well, this is my last "Mister Noah Time" with you children, but I'll be seeing you next week at the Lord's supper on Maundy Thursday. I love you. 'Bye-bye.

(Hands out animal tokens as children retreat. Traveling music.)

Maundy Thursday

Where's Noah?
Transition to "Where's Jesus?"

Mister Noah Time
Number Seven

Hi ho, everyone! Children, moms, dads, pastors! Captain, Mister Noah here. I'm back but not for long. My tongue says, "Hello," but tonight my heart says, "Good-bye." It's been a fabulous "Mister Noah Time" these past six weeks of Lent, hasn't it? (Messiah Lutheran) will never be the same. *(Laughs heartily.)*

It was terrific being able to share my story and how God saved me, my family, and all the living creatures on the face of the earth from certain disaster.

But now it's Holy Week and I must depart the stage. You have in the New Testament a new and better question to ask. Know what it is? I'll bet you do. It's "Where's Jesus?"

During Holy Week and now before you tonight on Maundy Thursday, we look towards Jesus, the Messiah of God. We meditate on Jesus and what he has done for us. Jesus saves you not from a flood of water but from the flood of sin and despair.

Have a wonderful time with Jesus and his disciples as you find him in the Upper Room. I bless you all as you celebrate the Lord's Supper. 'Bye now. *(Waves.)*

(Option: pass out a token of salvation, if it is available, or a final animal token.)

Ash Wednesday
Meditation

Where's Noah?
In The Swill!

Joel 2:12, 13

Friends in Christ Jesus our Lord,

Lent is checkup time.

A young fellow telephoned the druggist one morning and asked the question, "How's your new delivery boy doing?" "Fine," the druggist answered. "But aren't you my new delivery boy?" "I am, sir," the boy replied. "I was just checking up on myself" (*Seeds from the Sower*).

So did David in the Old Testament. He prayed in Psalm 139:23, "Search me, O God, and know my every thought."

Tonight we weave two Lenten strands together — ashes and absolution. Confession and forgiveness.

In the first place — ashes.

This Lenten Season we are asking the question, "Where's Noah?" It's a strange question, an unusual question, but certainly a necessary one for our day. Each week asking, "Where's Noah?" will help us inquire, not only, "Where is the biblical Noah?" or "Where is the dramatized Noah?" but probing more deeply, "Where are you and where am I as modern sons and daughters of Noah?"

When we ask the question, "Where is Noah?" tonight, we get an answer borrowed from the farm — Noah is in the swill. Noah in the swill? ... Swill? What may I ask does that mean?

Allow me to explain. I remember when Dad would say to me on the farm, sometimes after dark, "Son, go swill the hogs." He meant go "slop" the hogs. Swill, slop meant the same thing. It was liquified garbage, table scraps mixed with ground up screenings that the pigs relished. It was a messy job there in the dark amidst the grunts and the squeals and the pushing and the shoving.

In Genesis 6 we find Noah in an entire culture of swill and slop. It is dark morally. Bankrupt spiritually. The Bible says, "The Lord saw that the wickedness of humankind was great in the earth, and that every inclination of the thoughts of their hearts was only evil continually" (Genesis 6:5 *NRSV*).

The Apostle Paul described the human situation this way in Romans 1:28 ff: "And since they did not see fit to acknowledge God, God gave them up to a debased mind and to things that should not be done. They were filled with every kind of wickedness, evil, covetousness, malice. Full of envy, murder, strife, deceit, craftiness, they are gossips, slanderers, God-haters, insolent, haughty, boastful, inventors of evil, rebellious toward parents, foolish, faithless, heartless, ruthless. They know God's decree that those who practice such things deserve to die — yet they not only do them but even applaud others who practice them."

Where's Noah? In the swill and slop of human sin! The saddest words in the Old Testament are this, "God was sorry that God ever had made humankind and put them on the earth" (Genesis 6:5, 6).

I remember the fear and uncertainty, as a child, watching my mother put black coverings on the windows at night. I asked why. It was during World War II and she said, "So the Japanese will not see our kitchen light and bomb us." Fire bombs were dropping in South Dakota at that time, launched by helium balloons swept in by the jet stream from the west. Darkness may have been our safety, but the apprehension and insecurity were oppressive.

It was a spiritual, moral blackout in Noah's day, in fact, of such magnitude that Jesus refers to it in the Gospels. "As in the days of Noah ... so it would be when the Son of Man comes again" (Luke 17:26 *NRSV*).

Many centuries after Noah, the prophet Joel would speak an enlightening message for dark times. "Yet even now, says the Lord, return to me with all your heart, with fasting, with weeping and with mourning; rend your hearts and not your clothing. Return to the Lord, your God who is gracious and merciful, slow to anger and abounding in steadfast love ..." (Joel 2:12 ff).

Tonight, ashes on our foreheads symbolize "return." "I am sorry, dear God, I am sorry, my dearest neighbor. Please forgive me my transgressions, my neglect, my offenses."

The devil has two lies he uses at two different stages. Before we commit a sin, he tells us that one little sin doesn't matter — no one will know. The second lie is after we've sinned when he tells us we're hopeless.

It's easy to be like the fellow visiting Las Vegas who called the pastor, wanting to know the hours of the Sunday worship. The preacher was impressed. "Most people who come to Las Vegas don't do so to go to church." "Oh, I'm not coming for the church. I'm coming for the gambling and parties and wild women. If I have half as much fun as I intend to, I'll need a church come Sunday morning."

Brothers and sisters, hardly the intent of God's grace — hardly the true meaning of ashes and repentance and sorrow.

"Return to the Lord your God..." Joel calls. We listen openly and honestly tonight so the Holy Spirit can work as we confess our sins.

Secondly, ashes leads to absolution.

Lent is the time we hear the words of forgiveness. What greater words can we hear as we prepare for Holy Communion tonight than "our sins are forgiven on account of Jesus the Christ. Come clean and be assured of your salvation."

Noah, get out of the swill! Noah, by the grace of God let God save you. And God made an everlasting promise that God would, and God did. Come to the Lord's Supper tonight — your first time or your one-hundredth. Receive the body and blood of Jesus and full forgiveness of all your sins. You are absolved by his grace.

Over twenty years ago the Brazilian government decided to turn a certain prison in its prison system over to two selected people. The two were Christians. The prison was renamed Humaita. Its policies and procedures were conducted on Christian values. Two staff and the inmates ran the entire prison. Chuck Colson visited the prison and made this report:

> *When I visited Humaita I found the inmates smiling — particularly the murderer who held the keys.*
>
> *Wherever I walked I saw men at peace. I saw clean living areas, people working industriously. The walls were decorated with Biblical sayings from Psalms and Proverbs ... my guide escorted me to the notorious prison cell used for torture. Today, he told me, that block houses only a single inmate. As we reached the end of a long concrete corridor he put the key in the lock, he paused and asked, "Are you sure you want to go in?"*
>
> *"Of course," I replied impatiently, "I've been in isolation cells all over the world." Slowly, he swung open the massive door, and I saw the prisoner in the punishment cell: a crucifix, beautifully carved by the Humaita inmates — the prisoner Jesus, hanging on a cross.*
>
> *"He's doing time for the rest of us," my guide said softly.*[1]

Ashes to absolution. You are absolved. You are forgiven. Come eat and drink. Amen.

---

1. Adapted from *Christianity Today*, November, 1993. Copyright 1993. Reprinted with Permission of Prison Fellowship. P. O. Box 17500, Washington, D. C. 20041-0500.

Lent 2
Meditation

Where's Noah?
Walking The Path Of Faithfulness

Genesis 6:7, 8, 9: "... Noah was a righteous man, blameless in his generation...."
Hebrews 11:7: "By faith, Noah ... became an heir to the righteousness that is in accordance with faith."

Friends in Christ,

Last week when we asked "Where's Noah?" our eyes were drawn to the artwork on the mural on our east wall. We saw a man and his family who lived in the swill and slop of sin, surrounded and almost smothered by the wickedness of humankind.

Tonight we ask, "Where's Noah?" And the answer we get is "He's walking the path of faithfulness."

How did Noah do it? How did he keep the faith? I don't know. It couldn't have been an easy walk of faith, surrounded and clawed at by every "evil inclination of human imagination." How did Noah do it? I don't know — but I do have a clue — a starting point. Let's begin with the Nature of God. What is God like? God is faithful!

"Thumb through the Concordance and you will discover the faithfulness of God to be a favorite theme of the Bible. It sings through the pages like the recurring melody in a symphony, over and over: "the faithfulness of God." "God is faithful" is the dominant note of the Psalms, the unwavering conviction of the prophets, the underlying assumption of all that Jesus taught about the Father's care. In the epistles, in more than a dozen places, someone is talking about the faithfulness of God, saying to Christian people, "Hold fast your faith without wavering, for he who has called you is faithful." God will not fail you. In God is no darkness, no wavering, no shadow of turning. You can count on God, put your whole trust in God's love, for God is God, utterly dependable.

Soon our family will be burning down our beloved old family farm house. It's been home to us all these years. On the living room wall Mom hung a brown plaque with gold letters. It said "Jesus Never Fails." I grew up with that message always hanging there. So when the ashes cool and the structure is gone I will still, among many memories, have that one, the one Noah too must have had hanging in his tent. "God Never Fails."

Now because God was faithful to Noah, Noah was faithful to God. The mystery writer to the Hebrews includes Noah in a long line of faithful believers and says "By faith Noah, warned by God about events as yet unseen, respected the warning and built an ark to save his household ... and became an heir to the righteousness that is in accordance with faith" (Hebrews 11:7).

A scholar dissected faith one day and laid out its anatomy. Faith has three parts. *Notitia, Assensus,* and *Fiducia.* 1) Faith is *Notitia*. Knowledge. Basic objective fact. The word "notice" comes from *Notitia*. Faith does not begin with emotion. It's basis is the knowledge of God's love and faithfulness. 2) Faith is *Assensus*. Ascent, agreement, affirmation. We ratify, we approve, we concur. *Assensus*. Yes. 3) Faith is *Fiducia*.

Fiducia is a banking term. *Fiducia* means you have access to estates, bequests. It's an inheritance held in trust that is yours and mine. So faith is Notitia, Assensus, and Fiducia. But if you can't remember all that think of faith as a daring leap. A bungee jump. Leaping into the unknown but trusting to be caught and saved. Noah entrusted himself totally to God. And he did as God commanded.

One of the great leaps of faith in human history took place in 1960.

> *Alone in an open gondola of his balloon 102,800 feet above the New Mexico desert, Captain Joseph W. Kittinger, Jr., of the United States Air Force uttered a simple prayer: "Lord, take care of me now." Then he jumped. For the next four minutes and 38 seconds, the pressure-suited aeronaut fell at speeds up to 614 miles per hour. Joe's descent slowed only slightly by an experimental six foot wide stabilization parachute that kept him from going into a violent and probably fatal spin. "I found myself on my back watching the balloon recede above me," he recalled. Earth, sky, and departing balloon revolved around me as if I were the center of the universe." At 17,500 feet, Kittinger's main chute deployed automatically. Nine minutes later, having shattered world records for highest ascent and longest parachute drop, he lay on a bed of grass, sand, and sage — uninjured and grateful."* (Source unknown)

"Lord, take care of me now." No doubt that was the prayer of Noah as he walked the path of righteousness and faith.

We started out tonight by rediscovering the song of Scripture that "God is faithful." Then to the melody, harmony was added — by faith Noah was a righteous man, blameless. We come to ask now what about us modern sons and daughters of Noah? Too often my faith is lame, hardly a leap.

Dr. Gerhard Frost reports a conversation in his book *Blessed be the Ordinary*. "She spoke of her church in anger — fire in her eyes: 'Believe me, the churches that are growing know how to draw people in; they give them what they want, answers, full and final answers!' 'Well,' I answered, weakly, 'doesn't that cater to the weakness of wanting things too neat?' I sensed that she wasn't satisfied. I know now what I should have said: 'With all those answers, where's the need for faith?' To traffic in simple answers — isn't that promising too much? Is this respect for truth — truth always unfolding, deepening, and reaching beyond? Where is the life of faith unless one follows where one cannot see and have never been?"

This Lenten Season we are seeing in Noah another. Noah is but a type of one greater. It is the faithfulness of the Galilean that enables us to walk the road of righteousness. By Christ's blood we are healed.

God calls us tonight to faithfulness. "Be faithful until death and I will give you the crown of life" (Revelation 2:10 *NRSV*).

In the museum in the 1880s town on Interstate 90 east of the Black Hills, I saw a *Ripley's Believe It Or Not* article in a picture frame. It was about a dog named Shep whose master died in Fort Benton, Montana. Believe it or not, the dog followed the body to the railroad station and for nearly six years thereafter met every train through that town awaiting the return of his dead master. Faithfulness.

Wherever we go and whatever we do, let our prayer be: "Lord, take care of me now." Amen.

Lent 3
Meditation

Where's Noah?
Building An Ark And An Altar

Genesis 6:14-22; 7:5; 8:20
Acts 5:27-32

Friends in Christ,

When we ask our Lenten question tonight, "Where's Noah?" we're amused and amazed to see a powerful, muscled man, sweating in the sun, hard at work. He's busy building two projects — an ark and an altar. The first is an ark. You can see the skeletal shape. Looks like the ribs of a great whale. It's a ship made of cypress wood, 300 cubits long and 50 cubits wide and and 30 cubits high. Three levels and a roof. A ship to save his wife and sons and their wives and to preserve the animal species of the earth. Oh, Noah, have you gone mad?

And the second project — *after* the flood, Noah would build an altar — an altar of thanks to God his redeemer.

Tonight we are struck again by the mercy and care of Almighty God for Noah and his family. All the details are there to preserve Noah's family and the animal kingdom.

Not only are we struck by God's wonderful providence but also by Noah's "O. T." By "O. T." I don't mean occupational therapy — but Noah's O. T. — Noah's *obedience* and Noah's *thankfulness*. Obedience and thankfulness are the two perfect responses to God's grace.

First obedience. Obediently, Noah built the ark. The Bible says simply,"Noah did all that the Lord commanded." And it wasn't easy. I think Noah struggled terribly. Noah must have prayed his heart out. How could he bring himself to do such a dumb thing? An ark in a bone dry desert! Well, my sisters and brothers, I'll tell you how. Noah *listened*.

Urban Holmes in his book *Spirituality for Ministry* says, "To obey is to listen." So to whom do we listen?

1) We listen first to God. To obey is to listen to God. To obey is to listen to God's Word and the preaching and teaching of it. Sometimes it's the still small voice amidst the swirling, whirling, crashing, bashing sounds around us and within us. Nevertheless we listen.

2) To obey is to listen to others too. I'm sure Noah listened to his wife. I hope she gave him sound advice. Once when we were lost in Chicago my wife shouted, "Follow that bus!" I followed it — into a bus terminal. No doubt Noah listened to his family about the whole project.

3) Did Noah listen to his neighbors? Noah had to be discerning because his neighbors considered him a raving mad baboon! Whom we listen to is crucial. How we listen is just as important.

A sociologist on an African jungle expedition held up her camera to take pictures of the native children at play. Suddenly the youngsters began to yell in protest. Turning red, the sociologist apologized to the chief for her insensitivity and told him she had forgotten that certain tribes believed a person lost one's soul if one's picture was taken. She explained to him in detail, the mechanics of the camera. Several times the chief tried to get a word in, but to no avail. Certain that she had put all the chief's fears to rest the sociologist then allowed him to speak. Smiling, he said, "The children were trying to tell you that you forgot to take off the lens cap." (Source unknown)

Ever feel like that? Like the chief and the children? Ever jump up and down to be listened to? It happens all the time. Someone said in memory of a friend, "His thoughts were slow, his words were few and never formed to glisten, but he was joy to all his friends — you should have heard him listen."

We obey only after we listen. Noah listened, obeyed, and built an ark. Noah's obedience gives us insight into Christ. Jesus, too, listened to his Father's word. Jesus obeyed the Father's will. In that great hymn to the Philippians Paul would write: "And being found in human form, he [that is Jesus] humbled himself and became obedient to the point of death — even death on a cross" (Philippians 2:7b, 8).

But, oh, it's hard to obey, isn't it? We've conveniently scratched "obey" out of our marriage vows. We have sacrificed obedience to the winds of whim and individual perogatives. Choices. Should we go shopping or should we go to church? Should we tithe or gamble? Too often obedience does not even enter the picture.

Tonight we applaud Noah for listening, and then obeying.

The second project Noah built was an altar. After the deluge they are a safe and grateful family. We read in Genesis 8:20: "Then Noah built an altar to the Lord, and took of every clean animal and offered burnt offerings on the altar ... and the Lord smelled the pleasing odor...." What a lovely picture. Think of the pleasing aromas that you love. Mom's freshly baked bread, popcorn at the theatre, the scent of sweet clover, the fragrance of perfume. Crisp mountain air. A hint of vanilla on a pine tree bark. Noah's thankoffering was like sweet perfume to God.

The Psalmist (136:1-9) said it and then sang it: "O give thanks to the Lord for he is good for his steadfast love endures forever...."

Izaak Walton once said, "God has two dwellings — one in heaven and the other in a meek and thankful heart."

Tonight, what comes to mind when you stand by your "Thank You" altar? What sweet incense rises up to God? In the beginning of books and at the end of movies are the credits. Lists of those to whom recognition and appreciation are due. What are your credits tonight? I have a few. I say thanks to the garbarge truck driver who didn't blow his air horn at me while I sat day dreaming through a green light. I say belated thanks to our retired postman who always delivered friendliness first and the mail second. I say thanks to my secret pal, a (Messiah) youth who gave me a valentine two weeks ago. I say thanks to thirty sixth graders at Garfield who made and sent valentine birthday cards to my 95-year-old mother, whom they don't even know. Most of all thanks to God's saving flood in baptism for making me God's child.

Where's Noah? Building an ark and making plans for an altar. And that's the way it is when God redeems and saves. Thank you. Amen.

Lent 4
Meditation

Where's Noah?
Saved On The Ark

Genesis 7:6-10, 23b
John 3:16

Friends in Christ,

Tonight when we ask the question "Where's Noah?" we are delighted to answer, "Saved on the ark." The Bible says the rains came and the flood rose and Noah, his family, and all the creatures of the earth were saved and safe on the great ship God had commanded Noah to build. Where's Noah? Saved and safe!

We see in this legendary story from Genesis 7 God's grace and preserving powers at work. The primary purpose of God is not only to create but especially to save.

A Baptist preacher walked up to me on the streets of Lake Benton one day and asked if I was saved. He was confident I wasn't. I mumbled something about trusting Jesus' death on the cross which was made personal in the covenant of my baptism. But he wouldn't accept my explanation. He was certain I was spiritually lost.

Saved! "Are you saved?" is a relevant question isn't it? It can be intimidating but it needn't be. To be saved means to be rescued from a terrible dilemma, preserved from an awful situation.

This past fall down south near Sherburn, Minnesota, two-year-old Walter Fuller got lost in an unharvested cornfield. One hundred fifty people began to search, and after eight hours fire fighters found him lonely, lethargic, and with low body temperature, but he survived. Walter was saved.

To lose a child is a nightmare but to find him is paradise. I remember the stark terror that went through me when our young son Joel was lost in Bandana Square in the Twin Cities. We searched and searched. Had he been abducted? Injured? We went crazy with worry. We were thankful when we found him idly inspecting an interesting display.

Some form of the word "saved" is found 296 times in the Old and New Testaments. It is the theme painted on nearly every canvas in the Bible. The poetry of the Psalmist sings of it. The parables of Jesus about lost coins, lost sheep, and lost sons proclaim the gladness of God when someone is saved.

If you want drama, read Dave and Barb Anderson's book about their rescue in the Bering Sea. They were on a mission in the far North. Their plane went down in icy waters, but they hung on to flotation devices and by several strange "coincidences" were found and rescued just in time. Their testimony inspires listeners to believe they were saved by the providence and grace of God.

Saved! When Christians say "Jesus saves," we mean saved *from* sin, death, and the power of the Devil. Paul wrote to the Ephesians, "For by grace are you saved through faith...." Luther explained further in the catechism, "[saved] ... not with silver and gold but with his holy and precious blood and innocent sufferings and death in order that I may be his own, live under him in his kingdom and serve him in everlasting righteousness, innocence, and blessedness.... This is most certainly true." Another way to say it is "Your debt is paid."

The Mayo Clinic in Rochester became famous because of the work of a father and two sons. William and Charles Mayo were like their father, physicians, as well as scientists and humanitarians. They published over 1,000 scientific papers about their work in medical journals. What they didn't tell people, however, was what they did behind the scenes for the less fortunate patients they cared for. As many as thirty percent of their patients were surprised and relieved to find handwritten words PAID IN FULL on the Mayo's bills — bills which they could not otherwise afford. And regardless of how much money the patients had, no one was ever charged more then ten percent of his or her annual income, no matter how expensive the treatment. And every dollar they collected on bills over $1,000 went to help other sick people. PAID IN FULL!

Now Noah was saved not just *from* something but *for* something. He was saved so that the family of God and the family of humanity might go on. He was saved so that God could enter into a covenant with him and eventually with Abraham and Sarah and Moses and King David. Noah was saved to point us to the ultimate new covenant in Christ the Savior.

Noah was saved for a second purpose. He cared for *all* Creation, not only a human remnant, but he preserved also the animals of the field and forest. Teachers of the scriptures in the '90s see this expanded purpose of Noah in John 3:16 and Romans 8:22. Start with John 3:16: "For God so loved the world that he gave his only begotten Son that whosoever believes in him will not perish but have eternal life."

The primary thrust of John 3:16 is God's love for people. But scholars note that the word for world in Greek is *cosmos*. For God so loved the *cosmos* ... The cosmos consists of all creation, not only human beings but trees, rocks, rivers, birds of the air, animals, fish, and amphibians. Christ loved and died for the entire planet.

Listen! Is it raining out? Do we face another kind of flood today? Is it of such magnitude that we are in denial of its very existence? Is it the ecological deluge? What are the signs? Some are saying, just as the canary was carried into the mines to give miners an early warning of deadly methane gas seeping into their tunnels, so the indicator species today, the mussel clams in the Mississippi, the songbird in the rain forest and the spotted owl in the western woodlands represent the same. These species are indicator species. They are sentinel species shouting alert, alert!

Tonight let Noah and the ark serve, not only as story of salvation from sin, death, and the power of the devil but also as a symbol of hope to inspire us to save our beloved homeland we call Planet Earth.

Are you saved? That's the first question. Everything else is irrelevant until that is clear. Then the second question comes into focus. For what purpose am I saved?

If not to save others and to save God's creation what else is there? Amen.

Lent 5
Meditation

Where's Noah?
Receiving A Rainbow

Genesis 9:8-17
Hebrews 10:23

Friends in Christ,

Over the past several weeks we have been searching for Noah and asking rhetorically, of anyone who will listen, "Where's Noah?" Some of the answers we have gotten to this question "Where's Noah?" are: in the swill, on the path of faithfulness, building an ark and an altar, and saved on the ark.

Now tonight we ask again, "Where's Noah?" And the answer is "Receiving a Rainbow."

The time is after the Flood. We find Noah with heart and hands wide open receiving two wonderful gifts: a promise from God and a lovely rainbow in the sky.

The first gift, a promise from God, is simply this: "I promise not to destroy the earth with a flood again. Never, never again."

"Promises and pie crusts," says an old proverb, "are made to be broken." That may be true for pie crusts, but not God's promises. The Bible is the promise book. It has been estimated that there are 30,000 promises in the Holy Bible. Psalm 146:6 testifies, "God is the God who keeps every promise" (paraphrased). Or as the *Good News Bible* puts it, "God always keeps his promises." 1 Peter 3:9 reassures us, "The Lord is not slack concerning his promises." And there is a wonderful Psalm, Psalm 105:42 which begins, "O, give thanks to the Lord ..." and why? For God remembered God's holy promises and for 45 verses the Psalmist praises God, recalling God's rescue and salvation of Israel.

The writer to the Hebrews in 10:23 writes: "Let us hold fast to the confession of our hope without wavering, for he who has promised is faithful."

God is our Promise Keeper. There is no other like God. We people break our confirmation vows, our marriage vows, our business contracts, our promisary notes to the bank, our New Year's resolutions, but God keeps every promise.

The instrument in the Scriptures to carry this promise is the covenant. God made promises sealed in covenants with Noah, Abraham and Sarah, with Moses on Mount Sinai, and with King David. And ultimately God sealed his promises in the New Covenant in the life, death, and resurrection of Jesus Christ.

The second gift Noah receives is a lovely rainbow. There it is in the sky. You see it and I see it. As a kid I always wondered *what* made a rainbow. I knew *Who* made the rainbow but I wondered *how*.

A meteorologist explains it this way: "A bow appearing in the clouds opposite the sun consists of the prismatic colors formed by the refraction and reflection of the sun's rays from drops of rain."

A poet would say: "Brushed on canvas sky, a brilliant splash of colors always surprising us after the dew and the rain."

After the flood, God consecrated the rainbow as the seal of the promise that God would not again destroy the earth by a flood. So the rainbow is a symbol of God's faithfulness and of God's beneficence toward humanity and all living creatures.

Now when you look at the rainbow I want you to note two colors: red and green.

The first color — red — let it represent the life-giving covenant God made with people, with human beings, with human life. "To you, Noah, and to your descendants I will not destroy." To say it in positive language, "I, God, Jehovah, the Ultimate Promise Keeper, promise to sustain your life." Let red remind Christians of life and the life blood of Jesus shed to save us from our sins. So we too, given life in our baptism, are called to be promise keepers. The great challenge is to keep *our* vows and promises and sincere intentions with our spouses, our family, all our people relationships.

The second color is green. Let green represent not only vegetation but all living creatures. "To you, Noah, and to your descendants and to all living creatures of every flesh I promise to keep and preserve the cosmos."

Last week we noticed that the ark contained not only eight precious people. It also contained the animals of field and forest. What a delight for us, adults and children, to bring all of our pretend animals of the ark here to the altar of God. It is not just cute; it is a holy moment affirming all God's creatures.

The Promise Keeper would have us rediscover not only people care and but also creation care. The crisis today calls us to covenant with the earth and with all living creatures.

"According to the Center for Plant Conservation, between 213 and 228 plant species, out of a total of about 2,000, are known to have become extinct in the United States. Another 680 species and subspecies are in danger of extinction by the year 2,000. The world's forests are being lost at a rate of 66 million acres per year, an area the size of Virginia and West Virginia combined."

The list of endangered animals both in numbers and severity grows alarmingly. The whooping crane almost went. In South India there is a preserve for the Nilgri Tahr, a rare and vanishing goat. One of these goats is at the zoo in Burnsville, Minnesota. Creation is threatened.

The Promise Keeper would have us become covenant keepers. Save the people. Yes! Share the Good News of the gospel of Christ so people may be saved from their sins. Yes!

Then also save the creation! Preserve all living things — the creatures of God's creating.

So tonight, we say, "Thank you, God, for the rainbow. For the red and the green." And for *all* the colors singing in harmony the song of confidence and trust: "We can depend on God our Covenant Keeper forever." Amen.

Lent 6
Meditation

Where's Noah?
Near The Saving Flood (Baptism)

I Peter 3:20-22

Friends in Christ,

This Lenten Season we are facing the growing threat of floods in our land. Already small tributaries, swollen by melted snow in the north, are racing south to gorge the larger rivers. And along the way these mischief makers — the Pomme de Terre, the Chippewa, the James, the St. Croix, and worst of all the mighty Red River — are raising havoc on small towns, farmland, county roads, township bridges, utilities, and entire ways of life. We have been made painfully aware of the destructive power of flooding water out of control.

There is, however, a bright spot in all of this. We have seen and experienced some wonderful human stories in the midst of the destruction. Without fail, crisis again brings out the best in people. The stories of sacrifice and heroism abound. Water has become the great equalizer. I have watched folks of every stratum of society, every age, race, religion, or profession, join hands and work together for the common good. You see them sand bagging, digging dikes, salvaging belongings, rescuing the stranded. I see weathly bankers shoulder to shoulder with the single mother on workfare. The work-release prisoner co-operating with the truant officer. Teenagers working and laughing along with the AARP folks.

Linda Francesco Bets asks in "Thinking about Water" in *The Lutheran Partners*, "Do we need such natural disasters to remind us how we are to live together and in relationship to God? Are the law, the prophets, and the good news of Jesus Christ not enough to teach us? Perhaps it is in the floods of life that we can most clearly see that God is in it with us — in my neighbor, in me, in the sandbag and the bottle of water, God chooses to be with us" (Jan/Feb, 1994, p. 31).

The Apostle Peter reminds us of both the destructive and saving natures of the flood in the story of Noah. "... God waited patiently in the days of Noah, during the building of the ark, in which a few that is, eight persons, were saved through water. And Baptism, which this prefigured, now saves you — not as a removal of dirt from the body, but as an appeal to God for a good conscience through the resurrection of Jesus Christ ..."

Surely, water angry and out of control drowns — but water tamed gives life and salvation as well.

Since our baptism we walk wet. Our walk does not end in drowning and death. The only drowning that takes place is the suffocation of the old Adam within us which must die to sin. Water kills, but water also gives life.

Paul wrote to the Romans, "For if we have been united with him in a death like his, we will certainly be united with him in a resurrection like his" (Romans 6:5).

Baptism is the "saving" flood because baptism connects us to the saving life, death, and resurrection of Jesus Christ.

I recall how precious water was when I was a young boy growing up on the farm in South Dakota. Dad and I hauled water in five-gallon cream cans from our neighbor's well. We had three shallow wells on the farm. We also utilized a cistern which collected rainwater from the house roof. My mother melted snow in the winter to wash clothes. Water was scarce. Water was precious.

Conservationalists and environmentalists are telling us we need to take a new look at our attitude towards this precious gift of God — clean, available water on the planet, before it is too late.

Now of course it is not only the water that saves. Martin Luther cleared it up when he wrote in the small catechism, "It is not water that does these things, but God's Word with the water and our trust in this Word. Water by itself is only water, but with the Word of God it is a life-giving water which by grace gives the new birth through the Holy Spirit."

1) Baptism as a saving flood offers a gracious washing. How good it feels to wash the dirt and grime from your face when you've been out in the dust and wind all day long. But then Peter says of this washing: "It is not a removal of dirt from the body but as an appeal to God for a good conscience" (1 Peter 3:21).

2) Baptism as a saving flood marks us. It identifies us. Baptism is God at work calling, choosing, marking us through God's Word. We belong to God. We are God's children bought through the blood of Jesus. We have been adopted by grace.

"But when the fullness of time had come, God sent his Son, born of a woman, born under the law, in order to redeem those who were under the law, so that we might receive adoption as children" (Romans 4:4, 5).

In the third serving of *Chicken Soup for the Soul*, George Dolan writes: "Teacher Debbie Moon's first-graders were discussing a picture of a family. One little boy in the picture had different color hair than the other family members. One child suggested that he was adopted and a little girl named Jocelynn Jay said, 'I know all about adoptions because I'm adopted.' 'What does it mean to be adopted?' asked another child. 'It means,' said Jocelynn, 'that you grew in your mother's heart instead of her tummy.' "

Long before you and I existed, God knew us, loved us, and adopted us as his children.

3) Baptism, the saving flood, sets us free. As Noah was saved — freed *from* the destructive flood — so he was safe, destined *to* serve and worship God.

Two little prepostitions — "from" and "to" — tell all.

"For you did not receive a spirit of slavery to fall back into fear, but you have received a spirit of adoption ... It is that very Spirit bearing witness with our spirit that, we are children of God, and if children, then heirs, heirs of God and joint heirs with Christ ..." (Romans 8:15ff).

Thanks be to God that by Christ's love and sacrifice on the cross made personal in our baptism, we are rescued *from* sin, death and the power of the devil in order *to* be free and share the hope of freedom to others. Amen.

Maundy Thursday
Meditation

Where's Jesus?
In the Upper Room

Luke 22:7-20

It was an Upper Room somewhere in the city. Perhaps a guest room. It was a pleasant place, where at eventide the cool breeze entered quietly and dispensed relief to its clients. You could find it too, up above the dusty, hot cobblestone street. Looking out at night you could see the twinkling lights of lower Jerusalem. And just now on the hillsides the sheep bells stilled and the marketplace asleep. Come on up! The room was ready. The table set. Flasks, goblets, clay plates laden with food. Unleavened bread and wine and bitter herbs and — a Lamb. The moment they entered, they would feel its welcome. Come on in.

It was just as Jesus had said. "A man and a jar of water. Follow him. When the man enters a house tell the owner the Teacher requests the guest room that we may eat the Passsover."

A bit later the rest of the disciples arrived. They looked about, saw the whitewashed walls, the latticed windows, the open veranda. They felt welcome. Took their places. The Passover Supper began. And as the evening unfolded, this special place where flickering candles cast quiet shadows on the walls, the Upper Room, was transformed into a place to remember and a place for love.

First — a place to remember. Jesus would commission forgetful followers to remember. Of course, they would remember the story of the unleavened bread and the passover wine. It had been taught to them. The bread of haste in leaving Egyptland. The lamb's blood the Israelites had painted on the door frames of their houses. That blood had kept death from their homes and saved their firstborn. Through lamb's blood they were delivered from Pharaoh's further foolishness and treachery. And for thousands of years Jews observed the Passover by sacrificing a lamb.

But when would enough blood be shed to fulfill the law? The question haunted them. Later the writer to the Hebrews shocked his Jewish readers: "... it is impossible for the blood of bulls and goats to take away sin" (Hebrews 10:4). Really, sacrifices of animal blood were only temporary solutions. Only God could offer the eternal one.

But now would they remember the New Covenant? Would they remember — when they were afraid how he stilled the storm? When they saw a leper — would they remember his compassion? When they saw a child — would they remember how he held one? When they saw a lamb — would they remember his face streaked with blood and his life flooded with love?

Jesus arose and spoke. All eyes upon him. "A new covenant I give you. I am the sacrificial Lamb. This cup is the new covenant in my blood poured out for you."

"Mommy, I'm so thirsty, I want a drink." Susanna Petroysan heard her daughter's pleas, but there was nothing she could do. She and four-year-old Gayaney were trapped beneath tons of collapsed concrete and steel. The worst earthquake in the history of Soviet Armenia took 55,000 lives. December 7, 1988, Susanna was trying on a new dress when the quake hit. Suddenly the nine-story apartment

collapsed and they fell into the basement — mother and daughter. Darkness. "Mommy, I need a drink. Please give me something." There was nothing Susanna could give. She was trapped flat on her back. A concrete panel eighteen inches above her head and a crumpled water pipe above her shoulders kept her from standing. Feeling around in the darkness, she found a 24-ounce jar of blackberry jam that had fallen into the basement. She gave the entire jar to her daughter to eat. It was gone by the second day. "Mommy, I'm so thirsty." Susanna knew that she would die, but she wanted her daughter to live. The two were trapped for eight days. Because of the darkness, Susanna lost track of time. Because of the cold, she lost the feelings in her fingers and toes. Because of her inability to move, she lost hope. "I was just waiting for death."

Susanna began to hallucinate. Her thoughts wandered. A merciful sleep occasionally freed her from the horror of her entombment — soon she would awaken to the voice of her daughter. "Mommy, I'm thirsty." At some point in that eternal night, Susanna had an idea. She remembered a television program about an explorer in the Arctic who was dying of thirst. His comrade slashed open his hand and gave his friend his blood.

"I had no water, no fruit juice, no liquids. It was then I remembered I had my own blood." Her groping fingers found a piece of shattered glass. Mother sliced open her left index finger and gave it to her daugter to suck. The drops of blood were not enough. "Please, Mommy, some more, cut another finger." Susanna has no idea how many times she cut herself. She only knows that if she hadn't, Gayaney would have died. Her blood was her daughter's only hope."[1]

"This cup is the new covenant in my blood," Jesus explained, holding up the wine. I must say to you, my brothers and sisters, I am thirsty. You are thirsty. Not thirsty for fame, possessions, passion, or romance. We've drunk from those pools. They are salt water in the desert. They don't quench. They kill.

But blessed are those who hunger and thirst for righteousness. Righteousness.

And the hand was cut and the blood was poured and the child saved.

"Remember — disciples — my blood of the new agreement shed to set you free from sin." So the Upper Room is a place for remembering.

Now secondly, the Upper Room is a place for love. The moon shone through the latticed window that night, a shaft of light pierced the gathering, and the room became a showcase demonstration of love. Then he lifts a towel and a basin and motions, "Give me your feet, yes, your tired, dusty, sweaty, smelly feet. Let me caress them and bathe them and kiss them."

Jesus continued, "And even now as I do this to you — do so to one another. My brothers and sisters, love one another."

And forever and ever this night in that Upper Room has become for them and for us the place and the night to remember and the place and time for love. Amen.

---

1. *The Applause of Heaven*, Max Lucado, copyright © 1996, Word Publishing, Nashville, Tennessee. All rights reserved.

Good Friday
Meditation

Where's Jesus?
At Golgotha

Luke 23:33
Mark 13:22

We're asking the question, "Where's Jesus?" on this Friday we call "good." We see him arriving at a hill place just outside Jerusalem.

The rapid events of the past hours — prayer in the Garden of Gethsemane, Judas' betrayal, Peter's denial, trumped-up charges of blasphemy, three kangaroo court trials, humiliation and torture — climax now in the ultimate insult, the Nazarene dragging two heavy timbers to a place called Golgotha.

This place in Hebrew was called, *gulgoleth*, possibly because Church Father Jerome thought it to be a place of unburied skulls. That place in Aramaic, the language Jesus spoke, was called *gulgulta*, possibly because it was a place of execution. Luke's Greek translates the place *kranion*. We get the English "cranial" or "skull" from *kranion*. Tradition has it that the hill looked like a ghastly skull. In Latin they called the place Calvary.

Whatever it is called, Golgotha was a place of death and desertion and there Jesus the Son of God was crucified.

Death by crucifixion was no doubt well known by Jesus. When he was a boy in Nazareth, the Jews revolted against the Roman oppressors barely five miles away, and Josephus, the Jewish historian, recalling this event, reports that the rage of Rome exploded and cruficied 2,000 revolutionaries along the roadway.

"The cross was Rome's ultimate deterrent, conveniently placed on the busy highways as a warning to all would-be rioters: 'Thus the enemies of Caesar are treated.' "

"Some years ago Israeli archaeologists discovered in a hillside cave near Jerusalem the first ever remains of a crucified victim from the time of Jesus. Though the bones had deteriorated, they were able to draw a rough sketch. He was a young lithe man, and the marks in the bones show that the nails were hammered into the forearms between the ulner and radial bones and not in the palms. Nails in the palms would be insufficient to carry the weight of the body, and would tear through them. The legs of this particular victim were twisted up and a seven-inch nail driven through the heel bones."[1]

The Jews themselves despised crucifixion. "Cursed is everyone who hangs on a tree," said the law (Deuteronomy 21:23).

Now Jesus, having been lifted up between heaven and earth, cries out on the cross, "My God, My God, why have you forsaken me?" (Matthew 27:46). With the sins of the whole world heaped upon him, Jesus feels totally abandoned. He *is* alone.

On this Good Friday we see *faces* and *places.*

Faces

Around the cross at a little distance are familiar faces. Full of love. Pained. Tear stained. Mary Magdalene; Mary, Jesus' own mother; and John, the beloved disciple; and the others. Faces looking up. Faces asking, "How could this be?" "What is happening here?" "Where's God in all of this?" Faces of the two criminals. Faces of the hardened soldiers who were just doing their job. Faces of the High Priest and leaders of the Jews who finally got rid of this blasphemous teacher. Faces looking up at the dying eyes of Jesus.

These are faces along with yours and mine that hunger and thirst for undeserved forgiveness.

One Face, the Face up high, is the only face on the planet that can deliver — and did. "Father, forgive them for they do not know what they are doing" (Luke 23:34 *NRSV*).

On Good Friday, I see places.

Places

I see many Golgothas. Places of death and atrocity.

Picture in your mind the place of Skulls in the past fifty to sixty years. You see the skulls of the Holocaust. Six million Jews. We dare not forget.

Cambodia. Pol Pot the henchman from Hell. Skulls of his own people everywhere.

Uganda. The evil dictator Idi Amin. Practiced genocide on his own people.

And Rwanda. We sat idly by while 700,000 Huitsis and Tutsis machete each other to death.

Golgotha is a place of many faces.

One face we must not see at Golgotha. It is the face of indifference.

G. A. Studdert-Kennedy said it:

> *When Jesus came to Golgotha*
> *they hanged him on a tree,*
> *They drove great nails through hands and feet,*
> *and made a Calvary;*
> *They crowned Him with a crown of thorns,*
> *red were His wounds and deep*
> *For those were crude and cruel days,*
> *the human flesh was cheap.*
>
> *When Jesus came to Birmingham,*
> *they simply passed Him by,*

They never hurt a hair of Him,
    they only let him die:
For (folks) had grown more tender,
    and they would not give Him pain,
They only just passed down the street,
    and left Him in the rain.

Still Jesus cried, "Forgive them,
    for they know not what they do,"
And still it rained the winter rain
    that drenched Him through and through;
The crowds went home and left the streets
    without a soul to see
Jesus crouched against a wall
    and cried for Calvary."

Where's Jesus? On dark Friday we call good — he's at Gulgoleth! He's there that you and I might be saved.

The hands of Christ
    seem very frail,
For they were broken
    By a nail.

But only they
    Reach heaven at last
Whom these frail, broken
    Hands hold fast.
    — John Richard Moreland

Amen.

---

1. *Sounds of the Passion*, David Owen, copyright ©1987, Augsburg Publishing Company. Used by permission.

Easter
Meditation

Where's Jesus?
In the Garden Of Resurrection

Mark 16:1-8

They expected no Easter celebration. No lilies trumpeting "Christ is risen!" No sunrise worship. No Easter breakfast.

Mary Magdalene, Mary the Mother of James, and Salome shuffled toward the tomb that grey Sunday morning. The last few days had brought nothing to celebrate. The Jews could celebrate — Jesus was out of their hair. The soldiers could celebrate — their job was done. But the women certainly couldn't celebrate.

Like a "B" horror movie we see the three dark figures in the mist approach the cemetery garden. But unlike a "B" horror movie they are not planning an exhumation or incantation. We hear them simply whispering to one another, "Who will roll the stone away?"

There was no forklift left by construction workers in the garden. No bulldozer in the area. Not even a crowbar. The soldiers were gone. And the muscle power of the disciples asleep. "Who will roll the stone away?"

It is then that Mark's Gospel reports the stunning news. When they looked up they saw with eyes wide open two remarkable, unbelievable, incredible things: the large stone capping the tomb shoved roughly aside and a messenger, a young man dressed in white, speaking: "Do not be afraid. He is not here! He is risen!"

This messenger sensed their fear. Fear had gripped them during the crucifixon. Now anxiously they wondered what would happen next. It is then they hear the calming voice from the cave, "Do not be alarmed; you are looking for Jesus of Nazareth who was crucified. He has been raised."

We know fear, don't we? Fear of the unknown. Fear of losing control. Fear of chronic illness. Fear of the growing power of the cults. We fear loss. We fear death.

Benett Cerf, who played on *What's My Line* and a few other television game shows some years ago, was asked what he feared most. He didn't answer at first. The rest of the panel members all discussed the question in great detail and came to a consensus: their greatest fear was fear of annihilation. (This was during the Cold War.) Finally, Benett Cerf, reluctant to open his soul so publicly, confessed his greatest fear was "not being loved." Ever worry about that? Afraid of not being loved or accepted? Afraid of rejection?

Aphobeo is the New Testament Greek for "Fear not!" At least 25 times in Scripture an angel or Jesus or a representative of God says, *Aphobeo* — Fear not! "Fear not, I bring you good tidings of great joy ..." Fear not. He is risen! Rejoice!

A pastor asked a group of second graders, "What did Jesus say right after he came out of the grave? "I know!" exclaimed one little girl. "He said, 'Tah-Dah!' " (*Joyful Noiseletter*, Easter edition).

Put that into poetry and you get:

*Along came Wayne who made it plain
we should boldly show our awe,
'cause Christ, who died and rose
for us, showed us a great "Tah-Dah!"
This great "Tah-Dah!" we're called to share
with laughter and some play.
As joyful children of our Lord.
Let's make him smile today!*
— from *Joyful Noiseletter*

Now we who know the end of the Easter story, we who have read the last chapter and celebrate the hope that is in the risen Christ, still approach the garden of Resurrection with the same question as those women. "Who will roll the stone away again for us?"

If the first stone is fear, the stone in the second place is the stone of doubt. Easter morning we get into the wrestling ring and our opponent is doubt. Is the Resurrection a fact or a wish? Is the Resurrection of Jesus and *our* Resurrection the hope we long for or is it a myth or worse is it a lie? And doubt pins us to the mat with a painful half nelson but then we break loose by the power of the Holy Spirit.

Former President Jimmy Carter tells in one of his writings of a prayer he once regularly prayed: "Lord, help me believe in the Resurrection."

On vacation in Arkansas, just for a lark, I jumped on my niece's trampoline. Amazing how you can push down and then suddenly sail into the air. Up. Down. Up. Down. It was a blast. But keep me off the trampoline on Easter. I can do without doubt, faith, doubt, faith, doubt, faith. Up. Down. UP. I prefer solid ground.

Dr. Gerhard Frost wrote of the Resurrection and a line in his text became the title of the pamphlet, "It had better be true." Frost wrote of a friend who met a friend in church, "... In the moment for exchanging the greeting of peace, he eagerly touched her arm, then as she turned, exclaimed, 'He is risen!' To his surprise there were tears on her cheeks as she said, 'He is risen indeed!' then added in a whisper, 'and it better be true!' She then informed him of her husband's recent death."

Today we pray God to banish our doubt in the face of death.

And then we ask, "Who will roll away the stone of silence?"

When the famous agnostic Robert Ingersoll died, the printed funeral program left this solemn instruction: "There will be no singing."

If you and I believe Christ is still dead then there can be no singing. No organ, no keyboard, no guitar, no flute nor trumpet.

But this morning we *are* singing. We break the silence into smithereens. The Earth sings all morning. Song after song. Worship after worship. In church after church. The victory of our God is sure. "And blessed are they that have not seen and have believed" (John 20:29).

He is risen! Death is dead. Jesus is alive.

The stone of silence is moved, destroyed, and is no more.

> *She was a Hanoverian Countess. If she was known for anything, she was known for her disbelief in God and her conviction that no one could call life from a tomb. Before her death, she left specific instructions that her tomb was to be sealed with a slab of granite; she asked that blocks of stone be placed around her tomb and that the corners of the blocks be fastened together and to the granite slab by heavy iron clamps. This inscription was placed on the granite rock:*
>
>
> This burial place,
> purchased to all eternity,
> must never be opened.
>
>
> *All that any person could do to seal the tomb was done. The Countess had insured that her tomb would serve as a mockery to the belief in the Resurrection. A small birch tree, however, had other plans. Its root found its way between the slabs and grew deep into the ground. Over the years it forced its way until the iron clamps popped lose and the granite lid was raised. The stone cover is now resting against the trunk of the birch, the boastful epitaph permanently silenced by the work of a determined tree — or a powerful God."* [1]

The stone of fear and doubt and silence has been pulverized! We are the "Tah-Dah" people. We are alive in Christ forevermore. He is risen. Alleluia! Amen.

---

1. *Six Hours One Friday*, Max Lucado, copyright ©1989, Word Publishing, Nashville, Tennesee. All rights reserved. Used by permission.

Lenten Eventide Worship
Versicle

O Lord, hear our cry and come to us. This night protect us from all e-vil, harm, and dan-ger.
Give to us your stead-fast lo - - ve. A - - - men. Thanks be to Thee.

Text: Arley K. Fadness, 1937-
Tune: Arley K. Fadness

The Rain Came Down
By Jeffrey H. Callander

[Guitar Capo on 20] © Copyright 1996

```
     C       G       Em7      Am
1. In the beginning of the earth all was good.
   C       G         Dsus4      D
Adam and Eve lived in the way that they should.
   C         G         Em7      Am
But sin broke the spell of our God's holy plan,
   C         G           Dsus4           D
And soon all the people began to worship the creations of man, until ...
```

Chorus
```
       Am
The rain came down as the cries went up
         C           Em7
from the people all over the earth,
       Am
to the one who fashioned and made it good,
         C         D
whose breath had given them birth.
            Am
But the tide had turned — the course was set;
         C          Em7
God's wrath would cover the earth.
         G          D
And the people who said that God was dead;
                Am
they saw that rain came down as their cries went up;
Am
rain came down as their cries went up.
```

2. God said to Noah, "Build an Ark out of wood.
Then take all your family in, for in you, I've seen good.
Your faith it has kept you from a fate worse than death.
The Ark will protect you, but there's a watery grave for the rest." And then ... **(Chorus)**

3. The rain continued forty nights, forty days.
All life was extinguished as the Lord mended earth's ways.
God gave them the rainbow as a sign from above,
That God would not cover the earth again with wrath but fill it with love, because ... **(Chorus)**

4. Brothers and sisters of the Ark, hear my plea,
to trust in the promise of our Lord, who sets us free,
from sin and dominion of the prince of the night.
Don't look to the darkness, but lift your heads up to the glorious light, because ... **(Chorus)**

The Rain Came Down
By Jeffrey H. Callander

[Keyboard Edition] © Copyright 1996

```
      D        A         F#m       Bm
1. In the beginning of the earth all was good.
   D        A         Esus4       E
Adam and Eve lived in the way that they should.
   D        A         F#m       Bm
But sin broke the spell of our God's holy plan,
   D        A            Esus4           E
And soon all the people began to worship the creations of man, until ...
```

Chorus
```
      Bm
The rain came down as the cries went up
         D              F#m
from the people all over the earth,
      Bm
to the one who fashioned and made it good,
         D            E
whose breath had given them birth.
         Bm
But the tide had turned — the course was set;
      D             F#m
God's wrath would cover the earth.
         A            E
And the people who said that God was dead;
            Bm
they saw that rain came down as their cries went up;
Bm
rain came down as their cries went up.
```

2. God said to Noah, "Build an Ark out of wood.
Then take all your family in, for in you, I've seen good.
Your faith it has kept you from a fate worse than death.
The Ark will protect you, but there's a watery grave for the rest." And then ... **(Chorus)**

3. The rain continued forty nights, forty days.
All life was extinguished as the Lord mended earth's ways.
God gave them the rainbow as a sign from above,
That God would not cover the earth again with wrath but fill it with love, because ... **(Chorus)**

4. Brothers and sisters of the Ark, hear my plea,
to trust in the promise of our Lord, who sets us free,
from sin and dominion of the prince of the night.
Don't look to the darkness, but lift your heads up to the glorious light, because ... **(Chorus)**

The Rain Came Down

Keyboard Edition   J. H. Callander

© Copyright 1996 J H Callander

Noah's Ark
Wooden Animal Tokens
Sample Instructions

Senior citizens making animal tokens and Mister Noah distributing them to children and youth at Lenten worships make for a beautiful intergenerational interaction. A typical set of wooden animal tokens using rubber stamps purchased at hobby stores may look as follows:

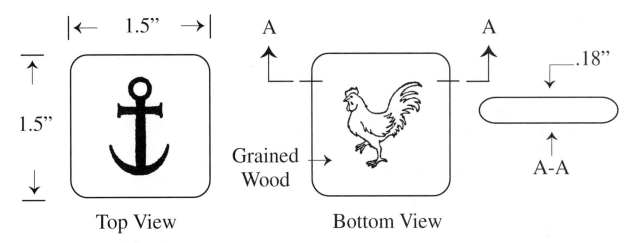

Noah's Ark
Animal Tokens
Scale: Full Size

Note: Using endangered species animals may help to intensify the care of creation theme.

"Mister Noah"
Character Guide

1. Select an appropriate actor who is comfortable in a public setting, likes children and youth, and can memorize the "Mister Noah" monologues. This "Noah" character needs to maintain a conversational style in the presentation and be able to ad lib as necessary.

2. The "Noah" character will be appropriately costumed with beard, sandals, gown, and turban. He may switch to a captain's hat.

3. The "Noah" character may promote the Lenten Series by appearing a week or two in advance, to the Sunday School and/or at Sunday and weekday worship services.

4. The animal token distribution may be supervised by Noah and implemented by the senior citizens of the parish.

5. The "Noah" character will serve as a bridge in the transition from Lent into Maundy Thursday of Holy Week.
   See the appropriate monologues for Maundy Thursday.

6. The Maundy Thursday Living Lord's Supper Tableau using the women's monologues and dialogues and accompanying worship outline may be considered an option. It is not required for a successful "Where's Noah?" series.

Crossword 1

Across

1) Appeared to Mary, Joseph, and the shepherds
5) Last book in the Old Testament
6) Key word from Mister Noah on Ash Wednesday
7) Matthew 5:1-12 are called
9) Person Jesus praises in Luke 21:1-4
12) "Jesus is _____"
13) _____ Magdalene

Down

2) Key character this Lenten Season
3) Noah's role in worship on Ash Wednesday
4) Symbol of God's Covenant with Noah
6) "_____" of the Spirit (Galatians 5:22-23)
8) David's occupation
10) God's chosen people
11) What Solomon is known for

Crossword 1 Answer

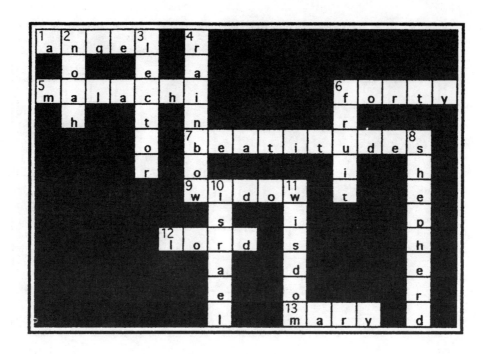

Crossword 2

Across

1) Shortest book in the Old Testament
4) His birthright was stolen
5) Characteristic of Satan
7) Jesus had twelve
9) Person Paul wrote his last letter to
12) First man
13) Key word from Mister Noah at Lenten worship #2

Down

1) Paul encourages children to do this in Ephesians 6:1
2) Wrote many Psalms
3) New Testament text for Lenten Worship #2
6) Author of Romans, the _____ Paul
8) Abraham's son
10) Bad guy in the book of Esther
11) Affliction of some men in Matthew 20:29-34

Crossword 2 Answer

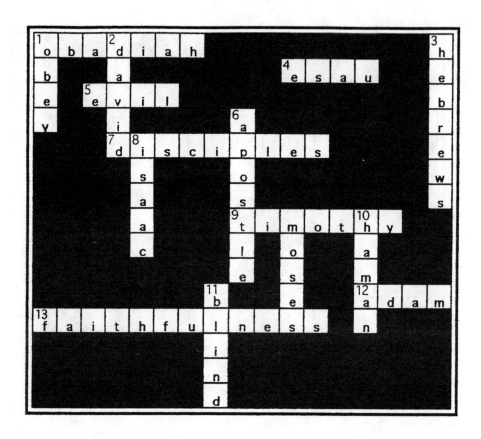

Crossword 3

Across

1) Betrayed Jesus with a kiss
3) Gospel writer
4) Key word from Mister Noah at Lenten worship #3
6) Tower of _____ (NRSV)
7) Shadrach, Meshach and _____
8) Protecting this is a key topic at Lenten worship #3
9) Jacob's favorite wife
12) The disciple whom Jesus loved

Down

2) Fourth fruit of the Spirit (Galatians 5:22-23)
5) An Old Testament ritual: Burnt _____
6) Ruth's husband
7) Arni was born _____ Hezron (Luke 3:33)
10) Love the Lord with all your _____ (Luke 10:27)
11) Disease in Matthew 8:1-4 (NRSV)
12) One of Jesus' close disciples

Crossword 3 Answer

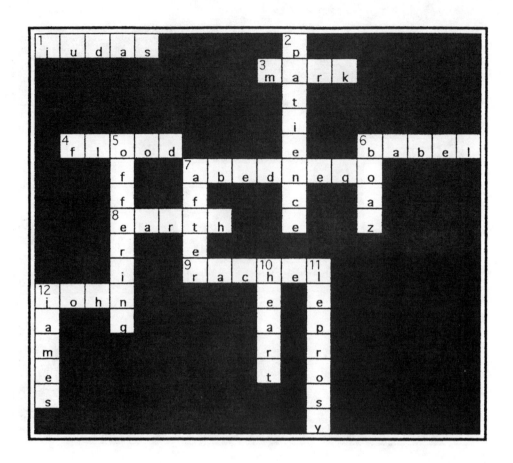

Crossword 4

Across

1) 18th book of the New Testament
6) Matthew's occupation
9) Noah's ride
10) Sea Moses crosses when leaving Egypt
11) Number of plagues God sends through Moses to Egypt
13) Key word from Mister Noah at Lenten worship #4
14) Second fruit of the spirit
15) Scripture text for Lenten worship #4
16) Synonym for key word at Lenten worship #4
18) Number of Jesus' disciples

Down

1) Jesus calls this person a rock
2) Only Gospel containing the lineage of Jesus
3) First Gospel in the New Testament
4) Key word in John 10:9
5) Key word in John 14:27
7) Alpha and _____ Revelation 1:8 (NRSV)
8) Quality of Jesus in Matthew 11:29
9) 44th book of the Bible
12) Love your _____ as yourself
17) Day Christians celebrate Christ's resurrection

Crossword 4 Answer

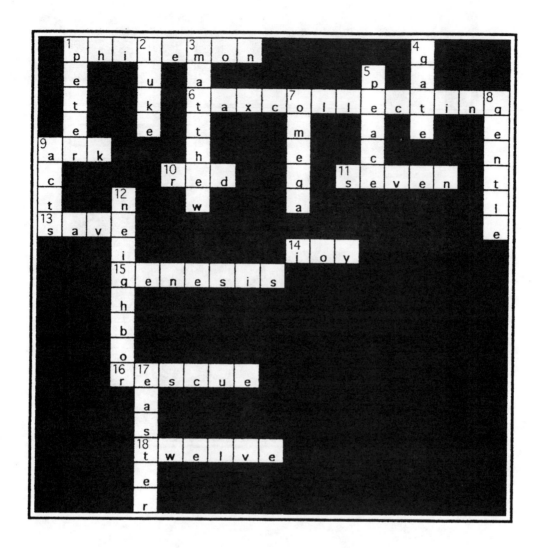

Crossword 5

Across

1) Key word from Mister Noah at Lenten worship #5
2) First major theme in Genesis
5) Faith as of a _____ seed (Matthew 17:20)
7) First woman in Genesis
8) Your body is a _____ (1 Corinthians 6:19)
9) Man leading army in Judges 7
13) Son of David and Bathsheba
14) Female prophet in Luke 2
15) Brother who tried to save Joseph in the Old Testament
16) Major traveling companion of Paul in Acts

Down

1) Theme for Lenten worship #5: _____ a rainbow
3) Jesus said, "I am the way, the _____, and the life."
4) Ham, Shem, and Japheth are _____ sons.
6) One of the books where the Ten Commandments are listed
10) First month of the sacred Hebrew calender
11) David's best friend
12) Joseph and Mary's home town

Crossword 5 Answer

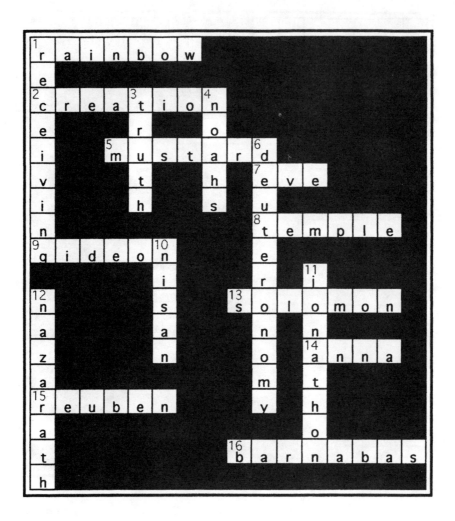

Crossword 6

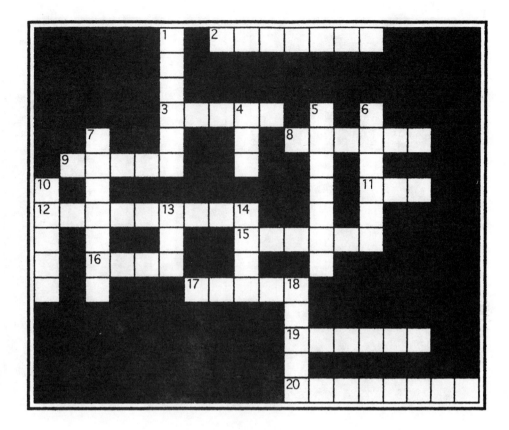

Across

2) Man who dies in Acts 5
3) Ishmael's mother
8) God sent Abram here
9) Physical element in Baptism
11) Jesus is God's _____
12) David committed adultery with her
15) First name of a Reformation Leader
16) Noah's son
17) Savior of the world
19) Animal symbolizing Satan in Revelation 12
20) Apostle who replaced Judas

Down

1) Reformation Leader
4) King of Judah who is committed to the Lord in 1 Kings 15
5) Noah's son
6) Lost his strength when his hair was cut
7) Key word from Mister Noah at Lenten worship #6
10) Abraham's birth name
13) Noah's son
14) Joel, _____, Obadiah
18) One of two famous evil Old Testament cities destroyed

Crossword 6 Answer

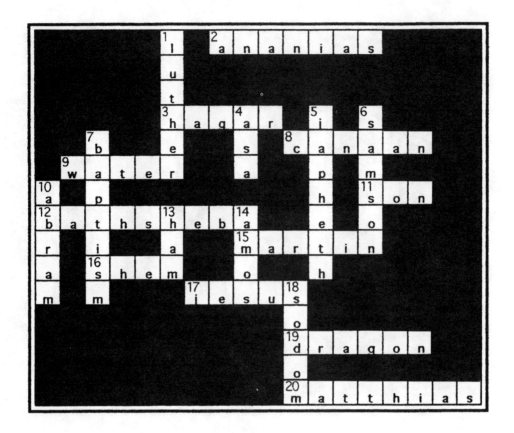

Sample
Letter To Parent(s)

Dear Mom, Dad,   Date, 2000

Paalleeese take me to Lenten worship this year!! Mister Noah from the Old Testament will be there for you and for us kids.

Mister Noah will teach us something very important, give us kids a wooden animal token from the ark and do a lot of fun, cool stuff.

Paaleeesse, let us go to church and worship God on Wednesday nights from _____ to _____ p.m. That's not too late. We can do it.

Thanks a lot,

Your loving child,

_____

Preparations For
Holy Communion On Maundy Thursday

1. Recruit:
   12 Disciples and Jesus (In costumes, nonspeaking parts)
   5 Women (In costumes, speaking parts)
       Mary Magdalene
       Martha
       Mary, Mother of Jesus
       Lydia
       Priscilla

   Duties Of The Five Women
   a. Hostesses and Servants
      Usher
      Take up offering
      Usher people forward for personal absolution
      Assist in communion as appropriate
      (Mary, the Mother of Jesus, will serve in place of Judas who leaves during the feetwashing ceremony)

   b. Speaking parts (see monologues)

2. Request the Board of Property to set up a Lord's Supper scene (backdrop) on the Tuesday before Maundy Thursday. Then, remove it before Good Friday worship on Good Friday. (You may wish to sketch an arrangement of how this will look in your chancel.)

3. Set rehearsal, robe preparation, makeup, and so on for Wednesday night before Maundy Thursday at 7 p.m.

4. Request Altar Guild to prepare the long "table" with candles, white cloth, stoneware-type dishes, plus the regular bread and wine for six stations.

5. Request choir or soloist to sing Richard Wilson's "Gathering Of The Disciples."

6. Secure bowl and towels for feetwashing ceremony.

Where's Noah?

A Bible Study
(Teacher Sheet)

Introduction
Where's Noah?" is a Bible study based on the legendary character, Noah, and his family, in the Book of Genesis. Genesis 9 dramatizes God's plan of salvation. The story also praises Noah's unquestioning obedience and sterling faith. This lesson compares Noah's experience of salvation with our salvation through Christ beginning in our Baptism. The promises of God in the covenant are the same as the promises in the covenant of our Baptism into the life, death, and resurrection of Jesus Christ.

Goals
1. The student will recognize God's loving desire to save and redeem humankind in the story of Noah.
2. Students will grow in personal faith and obedience to God as they link Baptism to salvation.
3. Students will be able to share a "rescue" experience they are familiar with. It may be someone's conversion to Christ, an animal saved at a humane society, or an environmental area preserved from destruction.

Bible Readings
Teachings in the story of the Flood include:
- God's faithfulness to a faithful Noah (Genesis 6:8, 14, 18; 7:1; 9:1, 8, 17)
- Noah is completely obedient and thankful (Genesis 7:5; 8:18, 20)
- Noah and his family, eight in all, are saved from the flood.
- God establishes a covenant with the rainbow as the physical sign.
- Peter 3:20-22, using the analogy of God's salvation in the flood, points to Baptism by Word and Water as a saving act.

How Does Genesis Describe Noah?
Noah is a picture of a most faithful, obedient man of God. Perceptive students of the Bible, however, may question Noah's behavior in Genesis 9:21. To be a person of faith does not mean to be sinless. It means to trust God in spite of one's weaknesses, faults, and sins. Daily repentance characterizes the Christian life.

What Was God's Covenant With Noah?
The covenantal purpose of God is to point believers towards newness. There is the new life in Christ and the promise of a new heaven and a new earth. (2 Peter 3:13)

How Does Baptism Relate To The Saving Experience Of Noah And His Family?
People baptized into the life, death, and resurrection of Jesus Christ experience salvation from sin, death, and the power of the devil.

Man Of Faith
In the Bible, the times of Noah were considered a time of extreme wickedness. The man, Noah, stands as an example of great faith and obedience. Noah was given outlandish instructions to build an ark on dry land. He nevertheless built it, because God commanded it.

Lesson Review
1. The Lord allowed the flood as a judgment upon the wickedness of humankind.
2. Eight people were saved.
3. Noah offered a sacrifice to give thanks and praise to God.
4. God promised to never again destroy all living beings by a flood, and to give the rainbow as a sign of God's promise and to bless all peoples through Noah.

More Learnings

A. Questions
- According to Jewish Law, certain animals and birds were considered clean or unclean. See the "Book of Laws" Leviticus 11:1-47, for a description of these animals and birds.
- Searchers continue to try to find the ark on Mount Ararat in the country of Turkey. Since the story of Noah is legendary, its historicity is difficult to identify.
- Noah is described as living until he was 950 years old. Legendary material in the Bible often uses large numbers in describing holy people involved in holy events.
- It appears that the writer of the Noah story used two different sources. That is why there are two different numbers of living creatures that entered the ark.
- The earth will not be flooded again. The Bible alludes to the possibility of destruction by fire (2 Peter 3:12). Christians focus, however, on preserving the earth while expecting new heavens and a new earth at judgment day (2 Peter 3:13).

B. Answer to puzzle:

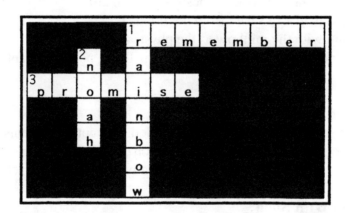

C. Assist the students in making a boat in an art form.

D. Youth see rescues on television. They know and read about animal rescues, protection of endangered species, recovery from human addictions as drugs, alcohol, work, sex, and other obsessions.

E. Give some pointers on how to write a skit. The skit can consist of a brief introduction, an emerging problem, and a solution.

Where's Noah?

A Bible Study
(Student Sheet)

Paid In Full

Three physicians, a father, William Mayo and two sons, Will and Charles Mayo, moved from Le Seur, Minnesota, to Rochester to begin the now famous Mayo clinic.

The Mayo brothers were scientists and humanitarians as well as visionary physicians. They published over 1,000 scientific papers about their work in medical journals.

Few people know that while they saved many lives, they also cared for the less fortunate. As many as thirty percent of their patients were surprised and relieved to find the handwritten words, "Paid in Full" on the Mayo's bills — bills which they could not afford. A patient was never charged more than ten percent of his or her annual income, regardless of how expensive the medical care.

Every dollar the Mayo brothers collected on bills over 1,000 dollars went to help other sick people.

Bible Readings

Read Genesis 6:5-9, Hebrews 11:7, and 1 Peter 3:20-22. Watch for the following words, images, and experiences:
- Faithfulness
- Obedience
- Saved From Destruction
- Covenant
- Rainbow
- Baptism

How Does Genesis Describe Noah?

The Lord was pleased with Noah in the midst of the swill and wickedness of humankind. God saved Noah and his family from the destruction of the flood. Noah was an obedient man of faith who trusted God.

What Was God's Covenant With Noah?

God made a covenant with Noah that there would never be a flood again that would destroy the earth. The rainbow would be the sign of this new promise.

How Does Baptism Relate To The Saving Experience Of Noah And His Family?

God saved Noah *from* the waters of destruction in the flood (1 Peter 3:20-22). So Baptism into the life, death, and resurrection of Jesus saves *through* the water and the Word. Read Martin Luther's water prayer in the baptismal service in the *Lutheran Book of Worship* page 122.

Man Of Faith

The story of Noah is presented in a literary form called a legend. A Bible legend is about holy people, holy places, and holy events. Noah's faith was the style of faith that trusted God completely without knowing the future circumstances, consequences, or end results. For Noah's obedience and faith he is listed among the model faithful in the book of Hebrews chapter 11. Noah received God's favor and blessing. Noah was chosen by God for salvation. Noah and all humanity received God's blessings through the covenant. Noah becomes a son and inheritor of promise.

Lesson Review

1. Why did the Lord allow a destructive flood to happen? _____
_____
_____

2. How many people were saved? _____

3. What did Noah do after the flood was over? _____
_____

4. What promises did God make to Noah? _____
_____
_____

More Learnings

A. Check questions you would like to discuss further with your teacher.

__ What is a ritually clean or unclean animal?

__ Will the ark ever be found?

__ How could Noah be so old?

__ Were there pairs of two or seven animals in the ark?

__ Will the earth ever be destroyed?

B. Fill in the crossword puzzle with key words in the Covenant with Noah.

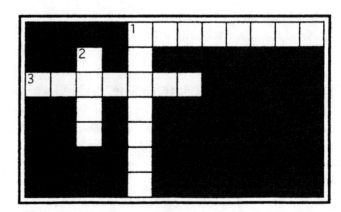

Across
1. Keep in mind (Genesis 9:15)
3. A commitment to be kept

Down
1. God's sign (Genesis 9:13)
2. Covenant was made between God and _____ (Genesis 9:8)

C. A boat or a ship is a traditional symbol for salvation. Do a "ship" art project in clay, newsprint, collage, wire, or some such medium. Display the artwork in a prominent place during the "Where's Noah?" series.

D. Participate in a simulated or real "rescue."

E. Write a skit and title it "911" about a rescue in real life.

Where's Jesus?
In The Upper Room

Monologue Number One
Mary Of Magdala

Good evening, I am Mary from Magdala. Martha from Bethany, Mary, the Mother of Jesus, Lydia, Priscilla, and I will serve as your hostesses and worship leaders in the celebration of Holy Communion tonight. Before you is the Upper Room and soon Jesus and his twelve disciples will gather there and we will celebrate the holy meal together.

They called me Mary Magdalene since I came from that region in Palestine — Magdala. It's on the southwest coast of the Sea of Galilee.

I first met Jesus when I really needed help. Seven evil spirits seemed to dominate my life. Jesus touched me and cast the demons out. I remember shouting, "Now I'm free! Thanks be to God."

I followed Jesus in his early Galilean ministry with Joanna, Susanna and others. I contributed financially to Jesus' venture. It was hard but I followed him to Jerusalem. I was present at the horrible crucifixion. Later I saw the empty tomb and was thrilled to see him alive again! Harlot I am not, as some labeled me. A credible witness of the Savior, I believe I am.

It was in this very Upper Room (motions to the Upper Room scene) prepared for the Passover Feast where the Master repeated the Great Commandment. You remember it. "Love one another even as I have loved you." Jesus then demonstrated that love by washing his disciples' feet and then instituting the Lord's Supper.

Tonight, as you Christians ask, "Where's Jesus?" you are fortunate to answer in faith — "Jesus is truly present in this Holy Sacrament."

But first let us prepare our hearts by beginning worship.

Please turn to King David's great Psalm of contrition and confession — Psalm 51, verses 1-13. We read this responsively.

Where's Jesus?
In The Upper Room

Monologue Number Two
Martha From Bethany

Hello. My name is Martha. I'm the sister of another Mary. She's not here tonight. My brother was Lazarus. Remember us? We lived in Bethany and many times Jesus visited us.

I was in charge of our household and served Jesus when he would drop by for a visit. I'd make him a lunch. Once I was busy in the kitchen and grew very impatient with my sister Mary for her doting on Jesus' little homilies. But afterward, Jesus spoke to me and I realized I was too involved with lesser things.

Yet they say I was a true follower of Jesus. When my brother Lazarus died and my sister was practically paralyzed with grief, I got up and went out to meet Jesus as he came down the road to Bethany.

I served Jesus and his disciples many times for dinner and for other needs they had.

Jesus loved all three of us so deeply. He even healed people like Simon the Leper right in my home.

Your tradition says I was a follower all right, even though at times I concentrated too much on secondary things. But I did my best, and I believe God our Creator was honored.

I was around when Jesus began to call women and men to follow him. He gathered twelve special people as his disciples and they joined him at that last Passover supper.

Where's Jesus?
In The Upper Room

Monologue Number Three
Mary, The Mother Of Jesus

My name is Mary. I am the mother of Jesus. You know me. You know me so well. I'm thankful and grateful and so humbled that God used me as a simple handmaiden to bring salvation to the world.

I raised my son in his childhood and I followed him in his adult life. Many times I was filled with joy and many times I was perplexed.

My son, Jesus, confused me that time in the temple when he was twelve years old and then later at the wedding at Cana. At times I felt anxious and worried. More often, though, I felt peace and calm from my God.

But the time that hurt so much was when I had to stand at the foot of the cross and see him tortured, dying — only 33 — so young — and I heard him tell John to take care of me. What a son — what a loss — I was so sorry — yet I knew in my heart something was coming.

I remembered the passage in Isaiah 61, when the prophet said, "... he has sent me to bring good news to the oppressed, to bind up the broken hearted, and to proclaim liberty to the captives ..." and then when God raised him from the dead I knew my son was the Good News.

Watch now with me, my sisters and brothers how he demonstrates the Great Commandment to love one another, by washing his disciples' feet in that Upper Room.

(Jesus washes the disciples feet; music background.)

(Judas leaves.)

Oh, look at him go. Judas Iscariot had made evil plans to betray Jesus to the Jews. He now knows it's time.

After Jesus washed his disciples feet, he began to speak:

(Pastor speaks the Words of Institution and leads in the Lord's Prayer.)

Where's Jesus?
In The Upper Room

Dialogue Number Four
Lydia And Priscilla

Lydia

When everyone had communed at that first Lord's Supper, they knew that they had proclaimed the Lord's death. They knew that this was the first installment of a wonderful banquet that would go on for centuries.

I'm Lydia and this is Priscilla.

Priscilla

Hello, everyone. I'm so happy to be here and worship with you. This is truly a wonderful night. I pray God's blessings upon us all.

Lydia

We celebrated the Lord's Supper in my home, too. My home in Thyatira was the first Christian meeting place years after Jesus ascended. The Apostle Paul stayed with us for a time. I am known as the woman who sold purple-dyed goods. It was wonderful to have the first Christians meet and worship in my home.

Priscilla

I was a leader in the new church, too. I was a tentmaker and teacher with my husband Aquila. We worked when the church was yet so small in Corinth and Ephesus and Rome, and now the Body of Christ has grown to millions. It has grown because the Holy Spirit has taught its followers to love God and to love one another.

The disciples you see up front are sitting there not because of privilege or status but because they were called to love and to witness. Their stewardship of love and life required the ultimate sacrifice — all but one would give their lives in martytdom.

Lydia

God calls you tonight, too, to words and deeds of love. Pray the Holy Spirit to lead and guide you to that end.

Now let us stand and sing, "Thank the Lord."

Sample Bulletin

Ash Wednesday
First Communion

Imposition Of Ashes

Prelude: "Are Ye Able" by Mason
"If I Have Wounded Any Soul" by Gabriel

Finnish Hymn: "Lost In The Night"*

Litany: Psalm 51:1-13 *(read responsively by verse)*
    Prayer
    Lessons*
        Genesis 6:1-7 *(The Wickedness of Humankind)*
        Joel 2:12, 13 *(Rend your Hearts)*
        Matthew 24:37-39 *(The Days of Noah)*

Sermon: "Where's Noah? In The Swill!"

Lenten Theme Song: "The Rain Came Down" by J. H. Callander*

Prayer

Institution Of The Sacrament

Lord's Prayer

The Distribution *(New communicants and families at the altar rail; Congregation at stations)*
    Special Music

Blessing

Song: "Precious Lord"*

Depart *(Leave offering at the door as you leave)*

Postlude: "My Heart Ever Faithful" by Bach

(Screen projection may be used here.)

Sample Bulletin For Lent

Lenten Vespers
"Where's Noah?"

Prelude: Water/Nature Sounds

Welcome

Versicle *(cantor ... congregation echo)*

Lenten Hymn*

Confession
Leader: Let us confess our sin in the presence of God and of one another.
(Silence for repentance)
Leader: Everlasting and forgiving God,
All: **I confess that I have sinned in thought, in my words and in my deeds — both things done and then left undone. I admit I have saddened and hurt you and my many brothers and sisters. I alone am responsible and beg your forgiveness so that I may know the peace and joy of eternal life. Give to me that courage to pass forgiveness on to others and make the necessary amends through Christ our Lord,**
Leader: Our God of mercy forgives you through the tragedy of Jesus' death and through the glory of his resurrection.
All: **Amen.**

Lessons*

Responsory: "Listen, You Nations"

Where's Mister Noah? Time

Lenten Theme Song: "The Rain Came Down" by J. H. Callander*

Sermon: "Where's Noah? ..."*

Offering: "Jesus, Remember Me"

Prayer: *Water Prayer* by Martin Luther

    Holy God, mighty Lord, gracious Father: We give you thanks, for in the beginning your Spirit moved over the waters and you created heaven and earth. By the gift of water you nourish and sustain us and all living things.

    By the waters of the flood you condemned the wicked and saved those whom you had chosen, Noah and his family. You led Israel by the pillar of cloud and fire through the sea, out of slavery into the freedom of the promised land. In the waters of the Jordan your Son was baptized by John and anointed with the Spirit. By the baptism of his own death and resurrection your beloved Son has set us free from bondage to sin and death, and has opened the way to the joy and freedom of everlasting life. He made water a sign of the kingdom and of cleansing and rebirth. In obedience to his command, we make disciples of all nations, baptizing them in the name of the Father, and of the Son, and of the Holy Spirit ...

    To you be given praise and honor and worship through your Son, Jesus Christ our Lord, in the unity of the Holy Spirit, now and forever. Amen.

Benediction

Lenten Hymn*

Postlude

(Screen projection may be used here. Add appropriate hymn titles and scripture texts for each service.)

Sample Bulletin

Maundy Thursday
Holy Communion Worship

Prelude: "Jesus Walked This Lonesome Valley" by Livingston, Jr.
"Ah, Holy Jesus" *(Herzliebster Jesu)* by Cruger

Monologue by Noah

Welcome by Mary Magdala

Litany: Psalm 51:1-13 *(spoken responsively)*

Lenten Hymn: "Hear, O My Lord"

Meditation: "Where's Jesus? In The Upper Room"

Confession Of Sins

Personal Absolution
*(Worshipers come forward and receive the laying on of hands. Respond with "**Amen.**")*

Nicene Creed

Offering: Solo — "I Only Want To Say" by Webber/Rice

Introduction: "Jesus Gathers His Servants" by Martha of Bethany

Song: "Gathering The Disciples" by R. Wilson from "He Lived The Good Life"

Monologue by Mary, the Mother of Jesus

Jesus Washes His Disciples' Feet
    Organ Interlude
    Judas Exits

Words Of Institution

Lord's Prayer

Distribution Of Holy Communion
    (Come to the stations at the table)
    Choir Anthem: "If We Truly Believe" by Don Besig
    Hymn: "Come Let Us Eat"

Blessing
    Our crucified and risen Lord, Jesus Christ, who now hath bestowed upon you his holy Body and Blood, whereby he hath made full satisfaction for all your sins, strengthen and preserve you in the true faith unto everlasting life. Peace be with you. Amen.

Narration by Lydia of "Thyatira" and Priscilla

Post Communion Canticle: "Thank The Lord"

Prayer

Benediction

Dismissal

Postlude: "Were You There?" by Smith

Sample Bulletin

Good Friday
"Where's Jesus? At Golgotha"

Tenebrae Worship

You are about to participate in one of the oldest forms of worship in Christendom. The worship begins with a fully lighted altar and sanctuary. As the passion story unfolds, the darkness increases as the candles are extinguished. With the death of our Lord, only one light is left burning — the light of God's love — the Christ Candle.

The Christ Candle will be carried out of the sanctuary and the complete darkness will symbolize the darkness of Christ's three days in the tomb. The Christ Candle is put back on the altar on Easter Sunday, symbolizing our Lord's victory over death — the Resurrection from the dead.

Prelude: "Ah, Holy Jesus" by Williams
"Beneath The Cross Of Jesus" by Maker

Lenten Hymn: "Beneath The Cross Of Jesus"

Confession Of Sins And Absolution
Leader: Let us confess our sins in the presence of God and of one another.
(Silence for self-examination)
Leader: Holy and gracious God,
All: I confess that I have sinned against you this day. Some of my sin I know — the thoughts and words and deeds of which I am ashamed — but some is known only to you. In the name of Jesus Christ I ask forgiveness. Deliver and restore me, that I may rest in peace.
Leader: By the mercy of God we are united with Jesus Christ, and in him we are forgiven. We now rest in his peace and rise in the morning to serve him.

Reading 1: Isaiah 53:2-6

Psalm Response: Psalm 22:1-8, 17-23

Hymn: "There's A Green Hill Far Away"

Reading 2: Hebrews 4:14-16; 5:7-9

Meditation For Reflection: "Where's Jesus? At Golgotha"

Offering: "Cross Of Sorrow" by Higgins

Shadows

The Shadow of Betrayal
    Bible Reading: Luke 22:1-22
    Special Music: "Ah, Holy Jesus" by women's trio
    Prayer
    Light Extinguished
    Bell Toll

The Shadow Of Desertion
    Bible Reading: Mark 14:32-50
    Hymn: "Alas, And Did My Savior Bleed"
    Prayer
    Light Extinguished
    Bell Toll

The Shadow Of Denial
    Bible Reading: Luke 22:54-62
    Hymn: "In The Hour Of Trial" (vv. 1-3)
    Prayer
    Light Extinguished
    Bell Toll

The Shadow Of Death
    Bible Reading: Mark 15:16-37
    Special Music: "Were You There?" by men's choir
    Light Extinguished
    Bell Toll (21 Fold)
    Stripping Of The Altar

Exit Christ Candle

Silence

Dismissal

Sample Bulletin

He Is Risen
Sunrise Easter Morning

The Announcement

Easter Hymn "Alleluia! Jesus Lives" (vv. 1, 2, 4, 5)

Adorn The Altar
  Remove the Veil
  Place the Lilies

Resurrection Dialogue
Leader: Alleluia, he is Risen!
All: **He is risen indeed!**
Leader: The great stone is rolled away, the tomb is empty!
All: **He is risen, Alleluia!**
Leader: Death has lost its stranglehold.
All: **And sin and Satan must forego,**
Leader: Their power and their bondage.
All: **Alleluia, he is risen. We've heard the Good News!**
Leader: Did you hear the Good News?

Welcome And Easter Greeting
  (Greet everyone with the words, "Good morning — he is risen!")

Song: "Lord Of The Dance" arr. by Sydney Carter

Prayer Of The Day
  O God, you gave your only Son to suffer death on the cross for our redemption, and by his glorious resurrection you delivered us from the power of death. Make us die every day to sin, so that we may live with him forever in the joy of the resurrection; through Jesus Christ our Lord, who lives and reigns with you and the Holy Spirit, one God, now and forever. Amen.

Special Music: "Was It A Morning Like This?" by Jim Croegaert

Psalm 150 *(unison)*
  Hallelujah! Praise God in his holy temple;
    praise him in the firmament of his power.
  Praise him in his mighty acts;
    praise him for his excellent greatness.
  Praise him with the blast of the ram's horn;
    praise him with lyre and harp.
  Praise him with timbrel and dance;
    praise him with strings and pipe.

> Praise him with resounding cymbals;
>> praise him with loud clanging cymbals;
> Let everything that has breath
>> praise the Lord. Hallelujah!

Drama: "Alive! An Easter Play" by Arley K. Fadness

Acts 10:34-43: *(Gentiles Hear the Good News)*

Song: "Rejoice In The Lord Always" (v. 1) by Ylvisaker

Colossians 3:1-4: *(The New Life In Christ)*

Song: "Rejoice, In The Lord Always" (v. 2) by Ylvisaker

Mark 16:1-8: *(The Resurrection of Jesus)*

Sermon: "Where's Jesus? In The Resurrection Garden"

Song: "I Will Dance With Jesus" by Ylvisaker

Affirmation Of Faith
    I believe in the living God the Father of humankind, who creates and sustains the universe by his power and his love.
    I believe in Jesus Christ, the man of Nazareth because of his words and work, his way with others, his knowledge of suffering, his conquest of death, his resurrection from the tomb. I know what human life is to be and what God is like.
    I believe that the Spirit of God is present with us, now and always, and can be experienced in prayer, in forgiveness, in the Word, the sacraments, the fellowship of the church. And in all we do. This we believe.

Offering: "Freely, Freely" by Owens

Offertory: "Thanks Be To God"

Prayers

Lord's Prayer

Hymn: "The Strife Is O'er, The Battle Done" (vv. 1 and 2)

Blessing

Hymn: "Let All Things Now Living" by Davis

Announcements

Postlude: "Christ The Lord Is Risen Today"

Fellowship Time

The Resurrection Of Our Lord
Easter Sunrise

Alive! An Easter Play

Texts: Acts 10:34-43 or Jeremiah 31:1-6; Psalm 118:1-2, 14-24; Colossians 3:1-4 or Acts 10:34-43; John 20:1-18 or Matthew 28:1-10

Theme: Prioritizing the Easter message over human traditions

Characters: Simon Peter (in costume)
Peter Cottontail (costuming that portrays a rabbit)

Tone: Serious, fanciful, and humorous. Appropriate for a youth Sunrise worship.

Synopsis: Simon Peter and Peter Cottontail, representing the sacred and secular dimensions of Easter, discuss their differences and come to a common understanding of the resurrection of Christ.

Setting: Garden scene

Props: Easter eggs, large carrot

Approximate time: 8-9 minutes

(Simon Peter is standing in the Resurrection Garden soon after the resurrection. It is dark. As the play progresses the lights come up until they are bright at the end of the play.)

Simon Peter: *(Soliloquy)* It seems like a dream. What the women told me. They said Jesus is alive. Risen from the grave, Oh no, I thought. That can't be. On Friday he was dead. Cold dead. No life in him whatsoever. I know dead and I know alive! He was dead. Yet those women persisted. "He's alive!" The other disciples and I thought it was an idle tale.

Nevertheless, I got up and ran to the tomb, right over there *(Points)*, stooped, looked in, and there I saw the linen clothes by themselves — no body — no Jesus. Suddenly I broke out in a cold sweat and my heart leaped — could it be? Could it really be? Then I remembered how he said that in three days he would rise. I never knew what he meant. Oh, my goodness! *(Clasps hands to face — Jack Benny style — though not for laughs. Face lights up and smiles broadly)* He is risen! He is alive! *(Does fast happy things like: takes lily from altar and gives it to a nearby worshiper, dances, skips, twirls gracefully, applauds, whistles or sings, and then stops abruptly)*

I am Peter the Rock! So they said. I often felt like Peter Pebbles. Doubting, skeptical, hardly believing the Master. And now Jesus is actually alive — risen from the dead by the power of God. Oh, my!

Peter Cottontail: *(From the shadows)* I might believe it!

Simon Peter: Whaa ... who's there? *(Lights come up on Peter Cottontail.)*

Peter Cottontail: It's just me. Peter. Peter C.

Simon Peter: *(Angrily)* That's *my* name! Are you mocking me?

Peter Cottontail: Oh, no sir, no sir!

Simon Peter: I've had enough to deal with *this* morning. Who are you or what are you anyway? A-a-a rabbit that talks? Oh, my lands ...

Peter Cottontail: Yes, I am Peter Cottontail. Everybody knows me. *(Turns to the audience.)* You know the song. Sing it with me. *(Sings)* "Here comes Peter Cottontail. Hopping down the bunny trail. Hippity, hoppity, Easter's on its way...." *(Hops about)*
    And here's another Easter song. *(Sings the Easter Parade song with the audience)*

Simon Peter: *(Interrupting)* What are you doing here anyway? This is a Holy Place. It's the tomb of Joseph of Arimathaea.

Peter Cottontail: Well, sir, I'm hiding Easter eggs so all the boys and girls can find them and ... *(Hides eggs)*

Simon Peter: *(Incredulously)* Easter eggs? Like what chickens lay?

Peter Cottontail: And people eat. Red, yellow, stripes, polka dots, all kinds — aren't they lovely?

Simon Peter: Well, I've got something much bigger on my hands this morning and I prefer to not mix up those silly traditions of yours with what seems to be the most incredible, unbelievable, unimaginable event that has ever happened in human history.

Peter Cottontail: And what's that?

Simon Peter: Jesus, the Christ, is alive! I saw the empty tomb where they laid him right here in the garden.

Peter Cottontail: *(Interrupts)* Who dyed the eggs? I did! *(Smiles proudly)* Who brought the jelly beans? I did! *(Smiles and bows)* And the chocolate rabbit? I did *(In a bragging manner)* And the Easter basket and the renditions of Easter Past? I did!

Simon Peter: *(Loudly)* But *who* raised Jesus of Nazareth from the dead?

Peter Cottontail: *(Meekly)* I didn't.

Simon Peter: Well ...?

Peter Cottontail: *(Protesting)* But aren't Easter traditions important!

Simon Peter: Like what? Your Easter parades with Easter bonnets?

Peter Cottontail: Yes, you bet!

Simon Peter: And egg hunts in the meadow?

Peter Cottontail: You got it, Rocky, ah, er, Peter, sir.

Simon Peter: Mr. Cottontail. What's important is this. Listen to what I wrote, years after that first Easter morning, to the exiles of the Dispersion in Pontus, Galatia, Cappadocia, Asia, and Bithynia: "Blessed be the God and Father of our Lord Jesus Christ! By his great mercy he has given us a new birth into a living hope through the resurrection of Jesus Christ from the dead ..." (1 Peter 1:3).

Peter Cottontail: A new birth! Like a new life? A new start? Dabba Dabba Do! But Mr. Simon Peter, what about all the Easter traditions and symbols accumulated over the centuries? Even you people like them. Even some who say they've experienced this, this, this "new birth," as you call it.

Simon Peter: Like?

Peter Cottontail: Well, like bulb flowers — Easter lilies?

Simon Peter: What do Easter lilies symbolize?

Peter Cottontail: I dunno. *(Crunches on a large carrot)*

Simon Peter: And chickens and rabbits and eggs and butterflies and robins?

Peter Cottontail: Haven't the foggiest.

Simon Peter: Those things are worthless if they don't point to this amazing event that I'm still woozy about. *(Holds head and sways a bit)* And if these traditions *help* us celebrate Jesus' resurrection from the dead, then let them be, Mr. Cottonfoot.

Peter Cottontail: *(Corrects him)* Mr. Cotton*tail*.

Simon Peter: Oh yes, Mr. Cottontail! Now let me teach you something about all this.

Peter Cottontail: *(Peter Cottontail sits at Simon Peter's feet)* Teach me.

Simon Peter: Well, the Easter lily is like a trumpet. It trumpets the wondrous news that Jesus is alive and well.

Peter Cottontail: I like that. *(Makes a trumpet sound with his hands.)*

Simon Peter: The next is the butterfly. The butterfly came through three stages of life. Caterpillar, cocoon, and then a beautiful butterfly like it was resurrected from the tomb.

Peter Cottontail: Oooo, that's terrific. I never knew that. What about the legend of the robin?

Simon Peter: Well, the legend of the robin goes like this: When Jesus died on the cross, a little robin noted that a thorn had pressed the forehead of Jesus, causing it to bleed. So the robin decided to fly down and pluck the thorn from Christ's head. But as the robin did this, a drop of Christ's blood fell on the bird's breast, staining it. From that time on, all robins have red breasts, so the legend goes.

Peter Cottontail: Oh yeah, it's a wonderful legend. It's *sooooo* beautiful. And what about the chickens and us rabbits?

Simon Peter: Not only are *you* God's creatures, but you stand for fertility and new birth.

Peter Cottontail: And the eggs?

Simon Peter: New life and the resurrection.

Peter Cottontail: Ohhh.

Simon Peter: You see, Mr. Cottontail — ah, er, Peter C., those traditions must never detract nor subtract from the main thing. They are useful only when they support and enhance the greatest joy of all — Jesus is alive!

So, go about your work, joyfully; hide those eggs and Easter baskets. And remember to sing. *(The two Peters walk off arm in arm, singing an Easter song.)*

The End

Outline For Screen Projection Option
Ash Wednesday Worship

**(Church Name)
Lenten Worship**

Ash Wednesday

Theme: Where's Noah?

"Lost In The Night"

Lost in the night do the people yet languish
Longing for morning the darkness to vanquish,
Plaintively heaving a sightful of anguish.
Will not day come soon?
Will not day come soon?

Must we be vainly awaiting the morrow?
Shall those who have no light let us borrow,
Giving no heed to our burdens of sorrow?
Will you help us soon?
Will you help us soon?

Sorrowing wand'rers, in darkness yet dwelling,
Dawned has the day of radiance excelling,
Death's dreaded darkness forever dispelling.
Christ is coming soon!
Christ is coming soon!

Light o'er the land of the needy is beaming;
Rivers of life through its deserts are streaming,
Bringing all peoples a Savior redeeming.
Come and save us soon!
Come and save us soon!

The Lessons
Genesis 6:1-7

¹When people began to multiply on the face of the ground, and daughters were born to them, ²the sons of God saw that they were fair; and they took wives for themselves of all that they chose. ³Then the Lord said, "My spirit shall not abide in mortals forever, for they are flesh; their days shall be one hundred twenty years." ⁴The Nephillim were on the earth in those days — and also afterward — when the sons of God went into the daughters of humans, who bore children to them. These were the heroes that were of old, warriors renown.
⁵The Lord saw that the wickedness of humankind was great in the earth, and that every inclination of the thoughts of their hearts was only evil continually. ⁶And the Lord was so sorry that he had made humankind on earth, and it grieved him to his heart. ⁷So the Lord said, "I will blot out from the earth the human beings I have created — people together with animals and creeping things and birds of the air, for I am sorry I have made them."

Joel 2:12, 13

¹²Yet even now, says the Lord, return to me with all your hearts, with fasting, with weeping, and with mourning; ¹³rend your hearts and not your clothing. Return to the Lord, your God, for he is gracious and merciful, slow to anger, and abounding in steadfast love, and relents from punishing.

Matthew 24:37-39

³⁷For as the days of Noah were, so will be the coming of the Son of Man. ³⁸For as in those days before the flood they were eating and drinking, marrying and giving in marriage, until the day Noah entered the ark, ³⁹and they knew nothing until the flood came and swept them all away, so too will be the coming of the Son of Man.

"Where's Noah? In The Swill"

"The Rain Came Down"

In the beginning of the earth all was good.
Adam and Eve lived in the way that they should.
But sin broke the spell of our God's holy plan,
And soon all the people began to worship the creations of man, until ...

Chorus:
The rain came down as the cries went up
from the people all over the earth,
to the one who fashioned and made it good,
whose breath had given them birth.
But the tide had turned — the course was set;
God's wrath would cover the earth.
And the people who said that God was dead;
they saw that rain came down as their cries went up;
rain came down as their cries went up.

God said to Noah, "Build an Ark out of wood.
Then take all your family in, for in you, I've seen good.
Your faith it has kept you from a fate worse than death.
The Ark will protect you, but there's a watery grave for the rest."

Chorus:
The rain came down as the cries went up
from the people all over the earth,
to the one who fashioned and made it good,
whose breath had given them birth.
But the tide had turned — the course was set;
God's wrath would cover the earth.
And the people who said that God was dead;
they saw that rain came down as their cries went up;
rain came down as their cries went up.

The rain continued forty nights, forty days.
All life was extinguished as the Lord mended earth's ways.
God gave them the rainbow as a sign from above,
That God would not cover the earth again with wrath but fill it with love, because ...

Chorus:
The rain came down as the cries went up
from the people all over the earth,
to the one who fashioned and made it good,
whose breath had given them birth.
But the tide had turned — the course was set;
God's wrath would cover the earth.
And the people who said that God was dead;
they saw that rain came down as their cries went up;
rain came down as their cries went up.

Brothers and sisters of the Ark, hear my plea,
to trust in the promise of our Lord,
who sets us free,
from sin and dominion of the prince of the night.
Don't look to the darkness,
but lift your heads up to
the glorious light, because ...

Chorus:
The rain came down as the cries went up
from the people all over the earth,
to the one who fashioned and made it good,
whose breath had given them birth.
But the tide had turned — the course was set;
God's wrath would cover the earth.
And the people who said that God was dead;
they saw that rain came down as their cries went up;
rain came down as their cries went up.

Celebration of Holy Communion

Hymn

Precious Lord, Take My Hand

Outline For Screen Projection Option
Typical Lenten Worship

(Church Name) Lenten Worship

Theme: Where's Noah?

Hymn

"God Is Here!"

The Psalmody

Psalm 36:5-10

The Lessons

Genesis 6:7, 8, 9

Hebrews 11:7

"The Rain Came Down"

In the beginning of the earth all was good.
Adam and Eve lived in the way that they should.
But sin broke the spell of our God's holy plan,
And soon all the people began to worship the creations of man, until ...

Chorus:
The rain came down as the cries went up
from the people all over the earth,
to the one who fashioned and made it good,
whose breath had given them birth.
But the tide had turned — the course was set;
God's wrath would cover the earth.
And the people who said that God was dead;
they saw that rain came down as their cries went up;
rain came down as their cries went up.

God said to Noah, "Build an Ark out of wood.
Then take all your family in, for in you,
I've seen good.
Your faith it has kept you from a fate
worse than death.
The Ark will protect you, but there's a
watery grave for the rest."

Chorus:
The rain came down as the cries went up
from the people all over the earth,
to the one who fashioned and made it good,
whose breath had given them birth.
But the tide had turned — the course was set;
God's wrath would cover the earth.
And the people who said that God was dead;
they saw that rain came down as their cries
went up;
rain came down as their cries went up.

The rain continued forty nights, forty days.
All life was extinguished as the Lord mended
earth's ways.
God gave them the rainbow as a sign
from above,
That God would not cover the earth again with
wrath but fill it with love, because ...

Chorus:
The rain came down as the cries went up
from the people all over the earth,
to the one who fashioned and made it good,
whose breath had given them birth.
But the tide had turned — the course was set;
God's wrath would cover the earth.
And the people who said that God was dead;
they saw that rain came down as their cries
went up;
rain came down as their cries went up.

Brothers and sisters of the Ark, hear my plea,
to trust in the promise of our Lord,
who sets us free,
from sin and dominion of the prince of the night.
Don't look to the darkness,
but lift your heads up to
the glorious light, because ...

Chorus:
The rain came down as the cries went up
from the people all over the earth,
to the one who fashioned and made it good,
whose breath had given them birth.
But the tide had turned — the course was set;
God's wrath would cover the earth.
And the people who said that God was dead;
they saw that rain came down as their cries
went up;
rain came down as their cries went up.

"Where's Noah? On The Path Of Faithfulness"

Hymn

My Faith Looks Up To Thee